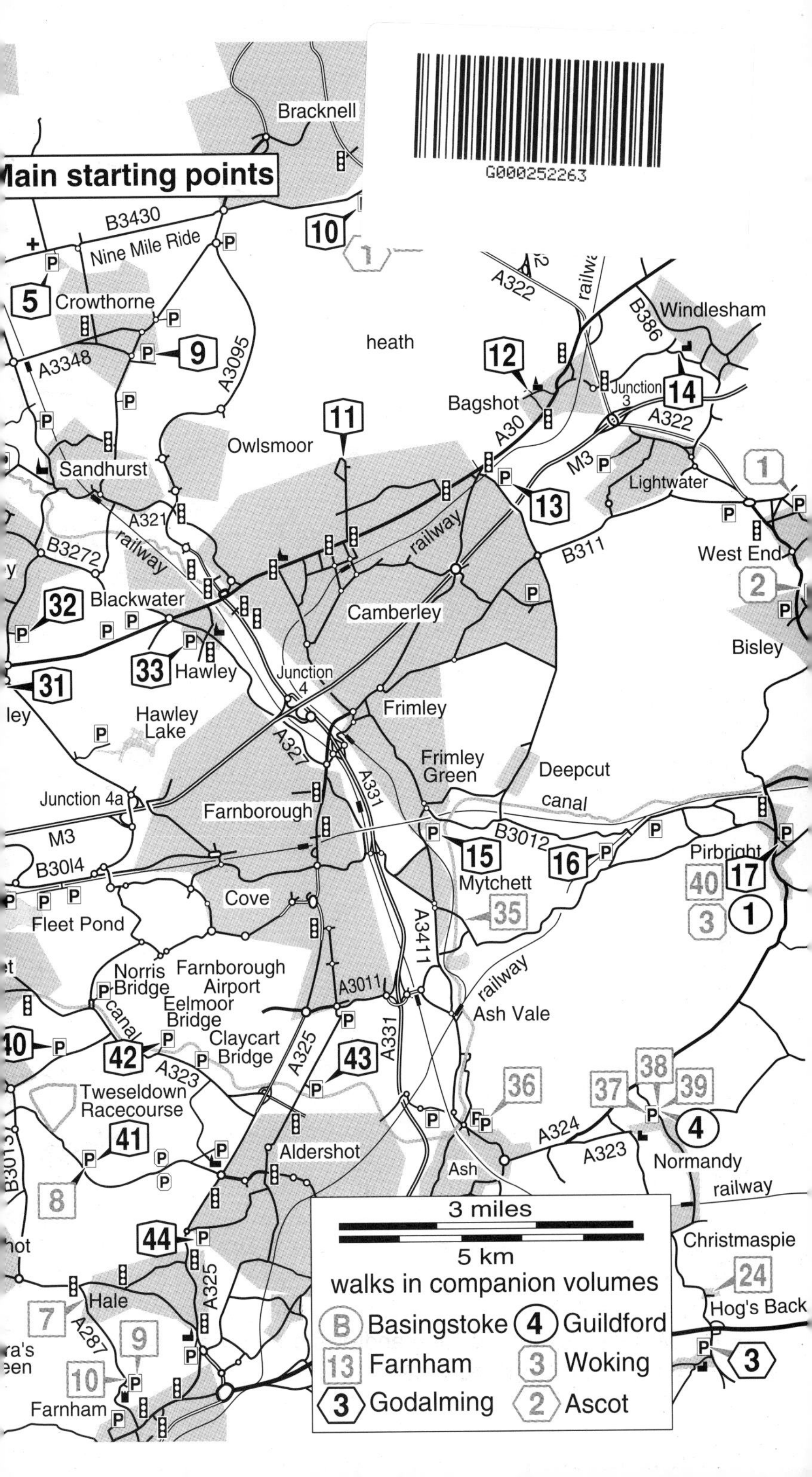

Main starting points
Bracknell
G000252263
B3430
Nine Mile Ride
Crowthorne
A3348
A3095
heath
Owlsmoor
Sandhurst
A321
railway
B3272
Blackwater
Hawley
Hawley Lake
Junction 4
Junction 4a
M3
B3014
Fleet Pond
Farnborough
Cove
A327
A331
Camberley
Frimley
Frimley Green
Deepcut
canal
B3012
Mytchett
A3411
Ash Vale
Norris Bridge
Farnborough Airport
Eelmoor Bridge
Claycart Bridge
A323
A325
A3011
Tweseldown Racecourse
Aldershot
A324
Ash
Normandy
Hale
A287
Farnham
Bagshot
A30
A322
B386
Windlesham
Junction 3
Lightwater
B311
West End
Bisley
Pirbright
Christmaspie
Hog's Back
3 miles
5 km
walks in companion volumes
Basingstoke
Guildford
Farnham
Woking
Godalming
Ascot

1 Swallowfield Park and Thatcher's Ford

About 7½ km/4¾ miles with an extension of 1½ km/1 mile; farmland and woods; undulating. OS maps 1:25000 159 Reading, 1:50000 175 Reading.

Start from Swallowfield Church, SU 732 647. There is parking in the village.

The Crown ☎ 0118 988 3260 ***The George & Dragon*** ☎ 0118 988 443[illegible]

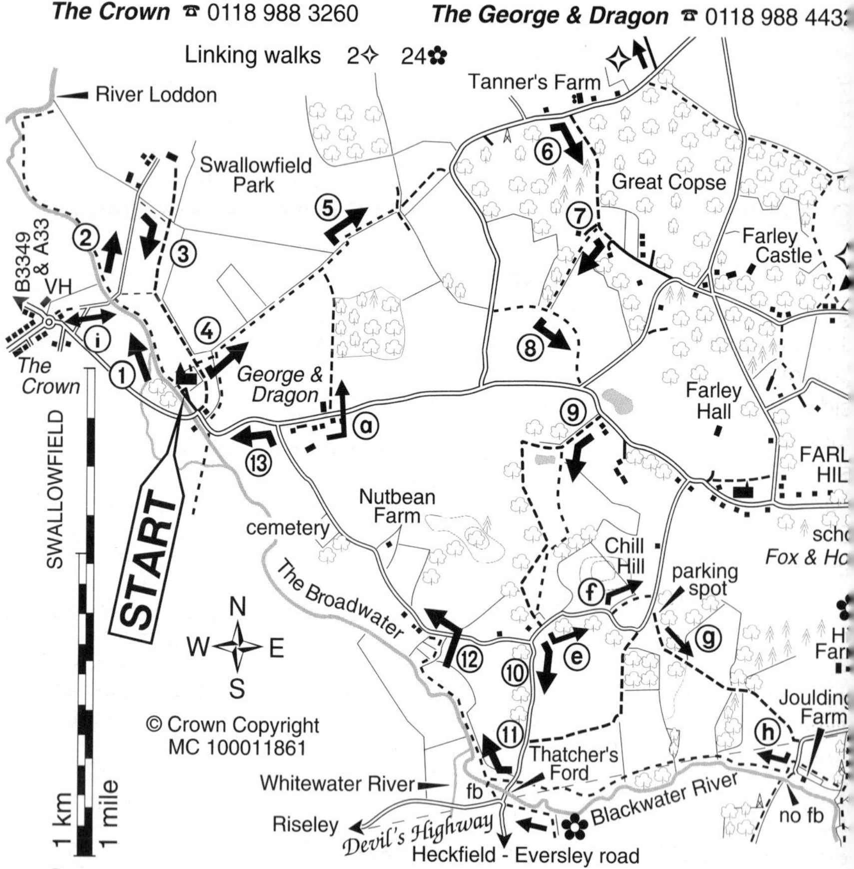

① From the inner corner of the car park at **Swallowfield** Church go through the trees to the field (20m) and on along the Blackwater **River** to the bridge (400m).

ⓘ *If visiting the village pub, cross the bridge. When the drive bends L stay ahead on the path past the lodge (200m) and the side road opposite to the* ***Crown*** *(150m). Return the same way to the bridge.*

② Follow the drive towards the big house, Swallowfield Park (350m).

③ Turn R along the garden hedge to the cart track (200m) and follow it back to the church (500m).

④ Opposite the churchyard R, turn L through the trees to the field (60m) and follow the L edge past a side path R (from the road at the ***George & Dragon***) (500m). Go on along the hedge to the gap (100m).

⑤ Continue on the other side to the end of the field (200m) and along the track in the next field, bending R to the road (300m) io on along the road L (350m). ✧ ioon after the timber-framed ouse L watch out for the forestry rack R (80m).

) Go up the track through Great ;opse to the flat top (300m) and he first house drive R (70m).

7) Take the path L of the drive own through the trees to the field 100m) and continue outside the ield to the bottom (200m).

3) Go L between hedges round to he road junction (300m) then L on he wider road curving R (120m).

9) At the next L bend turn R along he track between garden and field 200m). On the R curve take the ide path into the 2nd field L. Make or the highest point (300m). At the ummit spinney turn R down to the ear corner of the field (100m). Don't cross the track into the field ahead but enter the side field L. Nalk straight across the foot of the slope to the gate near the furthest corner and out to the lane (400m).

e) *Extension of 1½ km/1 mile: Walk L up the lane, over the top and down to the R curve (200m).*

f) *Turn off L up the stepped path. Follow the L hedge, until it bends and stay ahead to the lane (150m).*

g) *Turn R and diverge L down the track beside the wood. Keep on to the next lane (550m) then turn R to Jouldings Farm (80m).* ✿

h) *Just before the garden turn R into the field. Follow the footpath near the river from field to field (1000m) (on the line of the* ***Devil's Highway****) to Thatcher's Ford. Cross the lane.* ➔⑪

⑩ Walk down the lane R, and L at the junction, to Thatcher's Ford (550m). Enter the field R.

⑪ Walk through the field to the footbridge (100m). Don't cross but go on along the river (Blackwater) past the mouth of the Whitewater River (150m) and as far as you can go (400m).

⑫ Take the path up R (150m). Go L along the lane past the houses, round a bend at Nutbean Farm (400m) to the T-junction (500m).

⑬ Turn L for the church (400m) or

ⓐ Go R to the *George & Dragon* (150m) then follow the paths over the fields to the church (1100m).

The Blackwater River flows into the Loddon at Swallowfield. The **Loddon** rises from the chalk in Basingstoke and joins the Thames below Sonning. The area of the river and its tributaries constitutes the Loddon Basin.

The **Blackwater** was the main river in earlier times; its great valley and the masses of flint gravel transported by it provide the evidence. Early in the Ice Age it flowed from the chalk mountains of the Weald probably near Hindhead. Its present puny form is due not only to climate change but also to the loss of its headwaters, captured by the Wey which joins the Thames at Weybridge. The present-day Blackwater rises on Rowhill at Aldershot, and forms a few miles of the Hampshire boundary with Surrey and Berkshire. All of its water comes out of the Tertiary Sands with low calcium. In the planning stage the A331 was designated the Blackwater Valley Relief Road - apt for it sweeps through the great Ice Age valley.

The **Whitewater** River which joins the Blackwater near Thatcher's Ford rises from chalk springs near Greywell Mill and flows over the London Clay. It has a much richer fauna and flora than the Blackwater. Crayfish may be seen on the bottom. It has eight mills perhaps because it runs through farm country.

The River **Hart** starts from Crondall village pond and joins the Whitewater at Bramshill.

2 Arborfield, Great Copse and the Loddon

About 9 km/6 miles with a short of cuts of 1½ km/1mile or 4½ km/2¾ mile and an extension of 1½ km/1 mile through tranquil, gently undulating farmland and woods. OS maps 1:25000 159 Reading, 1:50000 175 Reading.

Start at Arborfield Cross car park on Swallowfield Road, SU 760 669.

The Bull ☎ 0118 976 0204
The Swan ☎ 0118 976 0475

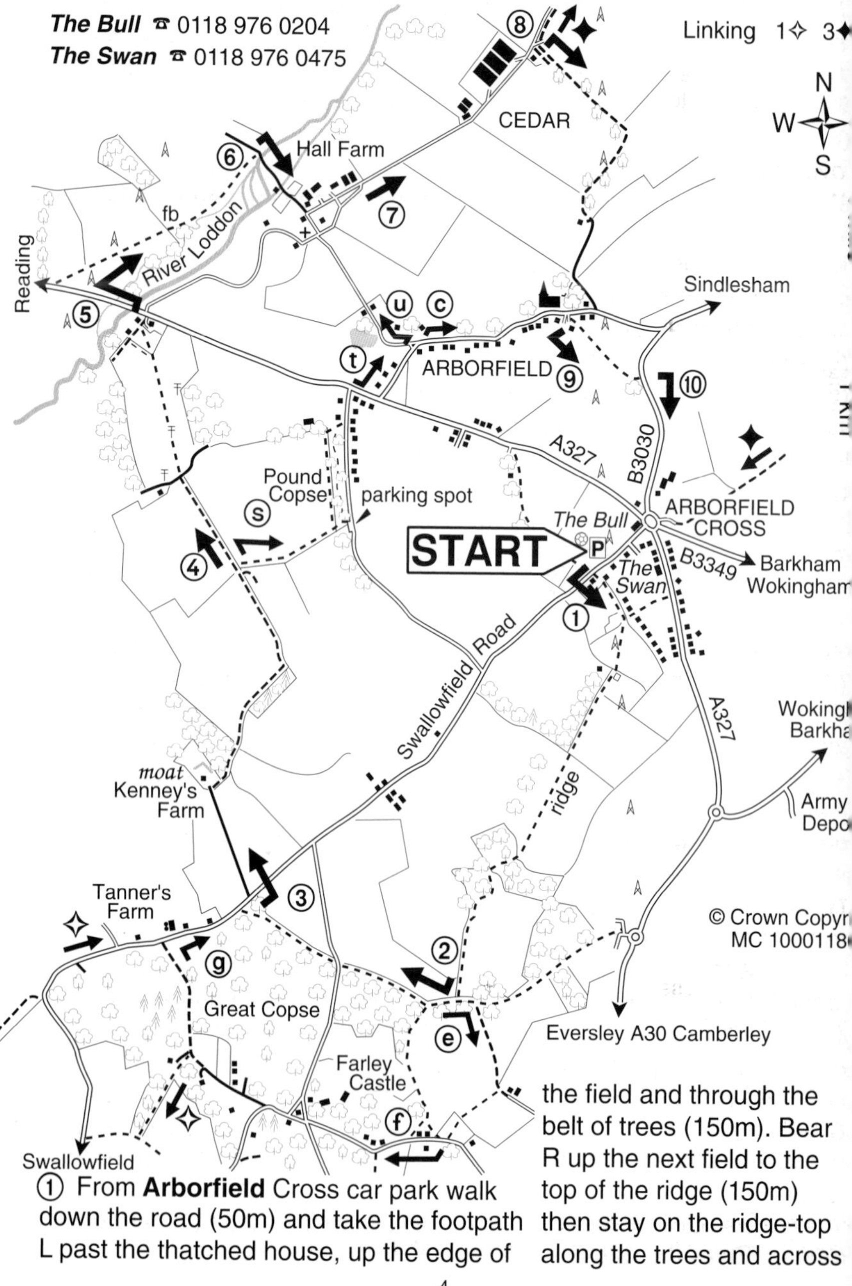

① From **Arborfield** Cross car park walk down the road (50m) and take the footpath L past the thatched house, up the edge of the field and through the belt of trees (150m). Bear R up the next field to the top of the ridge (150m) then stay on the ridge-top along the trees and across a field (700m). Go through the wood (100m) to the next field and on along the snaking R edge to the track in the belt of trees (500m).

ⓔ *Extension of 1½ km/1 mile: Go L on the track (70m) and take the side track R (300m). Just round the bend near the house, cross the fields R up to the lane (200m).*

ⓕ *Walk along the lane R (500m), over crossroads and on (150m). When the lane curves down L stay ahead on the level track to houses. Disregard side drives ✧ and drop off the **plateau** down the forestry track to the road (700m).*

ⓖ *Follow the road R (350m).* ➜③

② Turn R along the track to the lane (450m). Continue ahead to the next road (400m) then R (40m).

③ Turn L along the long straight farm drive (400m). Go round the corner near Kenney's Farm and on up into the large field (200m). Stay at the R edge to the corner (350m) and round L to the end (350m).

ⓢ *Short cut of 1½ km/1 mile: Just into the next field turn R into the side field. Follow the R edge to the corner at the wood (600m) then continue at the edge of the field or along the shady path in the wood to the end and out R (300m).*

ⓣ *Go L along the lane to the main road (120m), R on the pavement (100m) and L along Church Lane, opposite, to the bend (300m).*

(ⓒ *For the cut of 2½ km/1½ miles stay on the lane past the church (500m) to the path R (50m).* ➜⑨)

ⓤ *Turn L on the wide drive. Go round the bend and on past the Old Rectory to the cross drive near the ruins of Old Arborfield Church (400m). Take the next R.* ➜⑦

④ Stay ahead along the edge of the field (400m), over the house drive and slightly R along the middle of the next field (400m). Cross the next, little field, corner to corner, and go out R to the main road (150m) almost opposite the drive to Hall Farm (University of Reading). (This drive is used by walkers but there is no RoW.)

⑤ Go L over the **River** Loddon and on along the verge of the main road almost to the tree-lined end of the large field R (400m). Take the footpath back R across the fields, halfway between the pylons, from stile to stile (450m). After the foot-bridge keep to the R margin of the field to the hard track (400m).

⑥ Follow the track R over the Loddon and up to the farm road and house R (250m). Turn L.

⑦ Walk along the farm road (public footpath) through **CEDAR**. Arborfield church is visible far R. Carry on past numerous large barns L to the house R (1000m). ✦

⑧ Turn R on the track: not the one next to the garden but the one in the trees after it (20m). Stay on the track up round R & L bends to Monk's Cottage (900m) then up the drive to the lane (500m). Turn R to the footpath L (50m).

⑨ The footpath branches from a house drive near the stable drive. Follow it between gardens then fields to the B3030 (400m).

⑩ Go along the curving road R; there is more verge on the L side (450m). At the roundabout take the minor road, beside The ***Bull***, down to the car park (150m). (There is little path from the pub garden into the recreation ground.)

3 Arborfield and the Coombes

About 7 km/4¼ miles with an extension of 2 km/1¼ miles to Barkham, mainly on wide tracks; farmland and woods; bluebells in season; no stiles; undulating. OS maps 1:25000 159 Reading, 1:50000 175 Reading.

Start at Arborfield Cross; park in Swallowfield Road at the layby opposite the *Bull*, SU 761 670, or the car park 100m lower down. There are parking spots at Arborfield Church and beside Coombes Lane off Bearwood Road, SU 781 678.

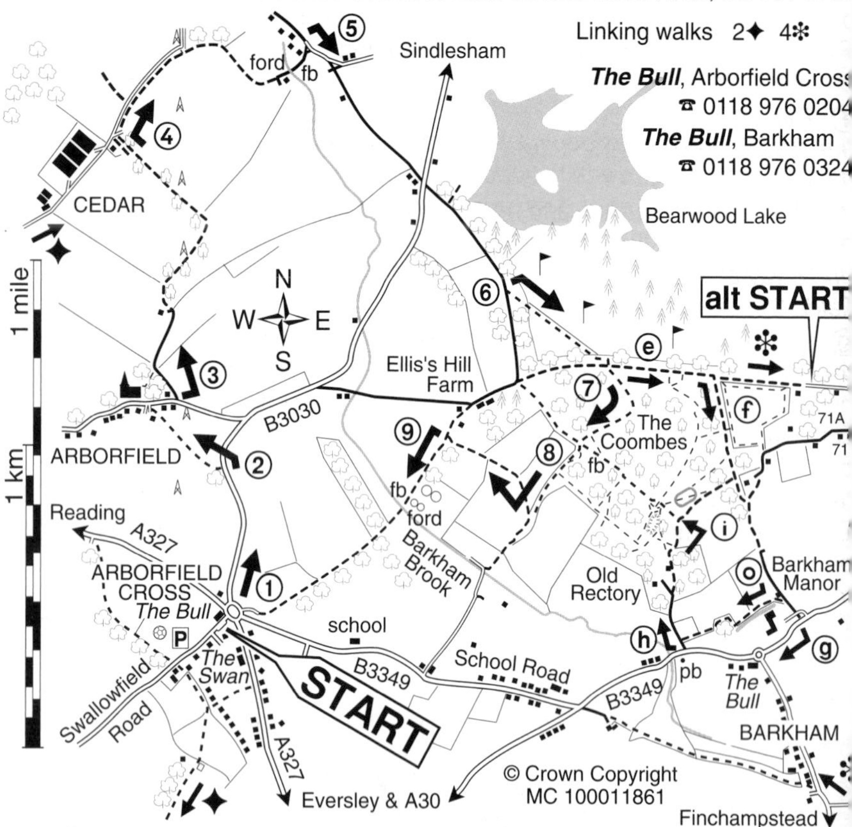

✦① From Arborfield Cross roundabout follow the R verge of the Sindlesham road (450m). Watch out for a footpath L on the R curve.

② Go along the footpath between fields and gardens to the road near **Arborfield** Church (400m).

③ Along the road R (50m) turn L down the drive to Monks Cottage (500m). Continue on the bridleway between fields to the concrete farm track of **CEDAR** (900m).

④ Bear R along the bridleway R of the concrete track. Stay on this bridleway round R, down to **Barkham Brook** (900m) and up the valley side to the lane (100m).

⑤ Turn R (60m). When the lane bends L stay ahead on the byway along the valleyside to the next road (550m). Cross and go up the hard track opposite (450m). Just over the brow and round a slight R bend, watch out for the side path L.

6) Take the side path through the belt of trees to the golf course (80m). **Bearwood** is visible above the lake and the pines. Bear R along the boundary fence of the golf course (300m). In the trees bear L (30m) and go out R to the byway, Coombes Lane (20m). ❇

e) *Extension to* **Barkham**: *Go L along the byway (400m).*

f) *Turn R on the track beside the first field R. Keep on ahead and off the hill (450m). After a house L join the converging track and go on down between paddocks to the bridleway at the bottom of the fields R (350m). Either ➔ⓖ or ➔ⓞ*

g) *Stay ahead to the road in the village (120m) and go along the pavement R to the* **Bull** *(200m). Continue in the same direction out of the village to the track in the trees R opposite a* **pillbox** *(250m).*

o) *(Very muddy when wet) Turn R along the bridleway past the manor to the track at the end (500m).*

ⓗ *Go up the track to the Old Rectory (200m). Continue on the horse track, up, round R and along the top edge of a field to the side path L at the twist (250m).*

ⓘ *Follow the side path into the wood (70m). At the lumpy ground (old gravel workings) look for the onward path (tricky) and follow it to the cross path at the corner of the next field (350m). Turn L. ➔⑧*

⑦ Almost opposite, take the path into the wood soon curving down R to a cross path at the corner of the first field R (400m).

⑧ Keep on down through the edge of the wood beside the field to the horse track (350m). Turn back R up between the fields to the ridge track near Ellis's Hill Farm (which has a farm shop and part time tea room) (400m).

⑨ Go L off the ridge into the valley of Barkham Brook (350m). Stay ahead up to the roundabout at Arborfield Cross (650m).

Bearwood is one of the grandest houses in Berkshire. It was built 1865-74 by John Walters III, to replace the house of his grandfather, John Walters I, founder of *The Times* in 1785. Now it is Bearwood College, a main-stream independent school. This was founded in 1827 as the Merchant Sailors Orphan Asylum in the City of London and became the Royal Merchant Navy School in 1921. A hunting lodge was here in ancient times and the name may derive from boar wood.

4 Barkham and the Coombes

About 7½ km/4¾ miles or a shorter version of 5 km/3¼ miles through the village; farmland and wood; undulating; bluebells in season. OS maps 1:25000 159 Reading, 1:50000 175 Reading.

Start from Barkham Church, SU 784 664, or a parking spot beside Coombes Lane, SU 781 678

Linking walk 3✻

The Bull ☎ 0118 976 032

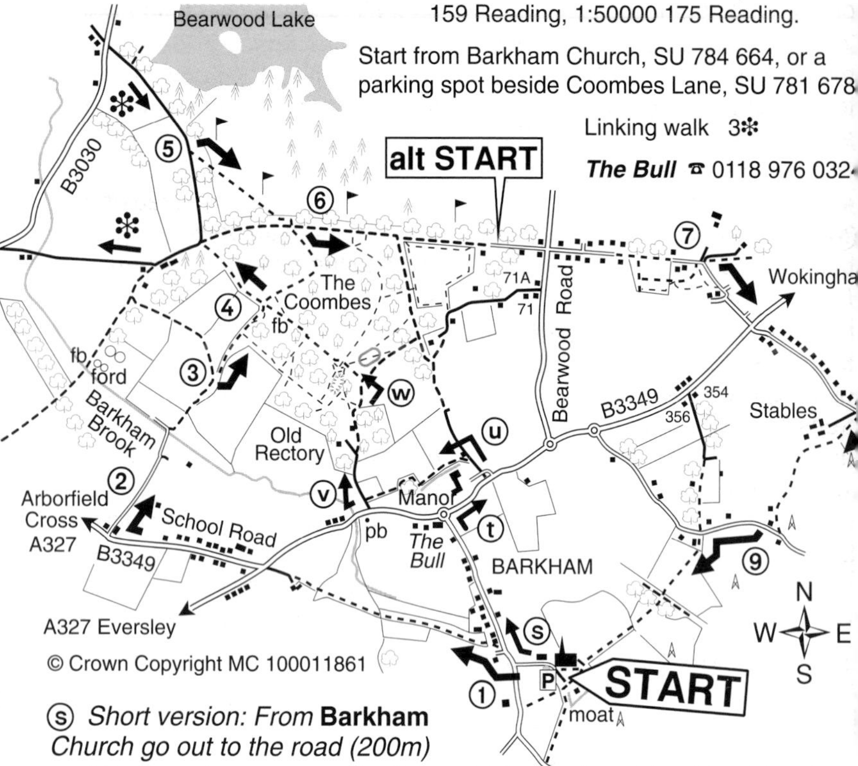

Ⓢ *Short version: From* **Barkham** *Church go out to the road (200m) and R along the pavement to the middle of the village (600m).*

Ⓣ *At the* **Bull** *cross the main road and go R on the pavement (200m).*

Ⓤ *At the end of the wall turn L. Cross the drive and follow the cart track (120m). After the garden take the bridleway L along the bottom of the fields past the manor house and stew pond, up round through the trees and on to the end (500m).*

Ⓥ *Go up the track past the Old Rectory (200m). Continue on the horse track, up round R and along the top edge of a field to the side path L at the twist (250m).*

Ⓦ *Take the side path through the wood (70m). At the lumpy ground (old gravel workings) look for the path ahead and carry on to the cross path at the corner of a field (350m). Stay ahead.* ➔④

① From Barkham Church walk ou to the road (200m) and R on the pavement to the 1st house (100m). Take the footpath L beside the house and go on along the L edge of the fields (750m). At the next house follow the drive to the road (100m). Cross and go along School Road opposite (600m).

② After the dip and R bend, turn R on Wood Lane. Follow the concrete track until it bends L (450m) then take the horse track R under trees between fields (250m).

③ When it bends up L join the footpath ahead. Keep on to the end of the L field (300m) and turn L on the cross path.

④ Go on at the edge of the wood, past the fields and up into the trees to the ridge track (300m). ❉ Stay ahead on the level track (300m) watching out for a side path R, 40m before the slight L bend.

⑤ Take the side path through the belt of trees to the golf course (100m). **Bearwood** is visible beyond the lake and the pines. Bear R along the boundary fence of the golf course (300m). In the trees bear L (30m) and go out R to the byway, Coombes Lane (20m).

⑥ Continue outside the golf course to the next field R (400m). Stay ahead on the track or walk along the edge of the field (250m). Go on past the Coombes Lane houses (300m), over Bearwood Road and along Sandy Lane (200m). After the houses descend the path ahead to the next road and keep on to the bend (300m).

⑦ Follow the roads down R to the main road (250m). Continue on the narrow lane opposite, almost to the power cables (500m).

⑧ Next to the drive to stables R take the footpath between the fields to the next lane (550m).

⑨ Walk along the lane R to the cross path at the R curve (300m) and turn L along the farm wall to the field (50m). Descend, slightly R (200m). Cross the farm track and belt of trees and go straight on from field to field towards the church spire (400m). Don't join the track, but cut through the church-yard (80m). Walk R of Church Cottages to see the moat.

The Domesday Book entry for Barkham - reproduced actual size

BERCHESCIRE.

TERRA REGIS.

Rex ten in dnio ~~Berchehā~~. Elmer tenuit de rege. E.
Te 7 m p. iii. hid. Tra. ē. iii. car. In dnio. ē una. 7 vi.
uitti 7 iiii. bord. cū. iii. car. Ibi. v. ac pa. Silua de. xl. porc.
Valuit. iiii. lib. T.R.E. 7 post 7 m. iii. lib.

The line through Barkham was in red for highlighting, not deletion. The script is easy to read. The Latin words are abbreviated uniformly eg Tra = *terra*, land; m̊ = *modo*, now. TRE = in the Time of *Rex* Edward ie before the Conquest. The entries were written on loose parchment skins in 1086 probably at Winchester where the Exchequer resided until the 13th century. The book is now on display at the Public Records Office, Kew. BERCHEHÃ was a manor, ie an estate, not a house or village. Forty pigsworth of woodland is larger than usual but a typical tax rating for a Windsor Forest manor.

BERKSHIRE.

LAND OF THE KING.
The king holds in lordship BERCHEHÃ. Elmer held it from king Edward
Then & now for 3 hides. Land for 3 ploughs. In lordship is one; 6
villeins & 4 bordars with 3 ploughs. There are 5 acres of pasture. Woodland @ 40 pigs
Valued £4 T.R.E; later & now £3.

5 Heath Lake and Lucas Hospital

About 8 km/5 miles with an extension of 2 km/1¼ miles via Ravenswood Village and a short cut of 2¼ km/1½ miles which may be used together; heath, pine plantations and woodland, almost flat, fairly shady. OS maps 1:25000 159 or 160, 1:50000 175 Reading.

Start from Heath Lake car park, SU 828 653, off Nine Mile Ride. In Wokingham the TESCO car park is close to the route.

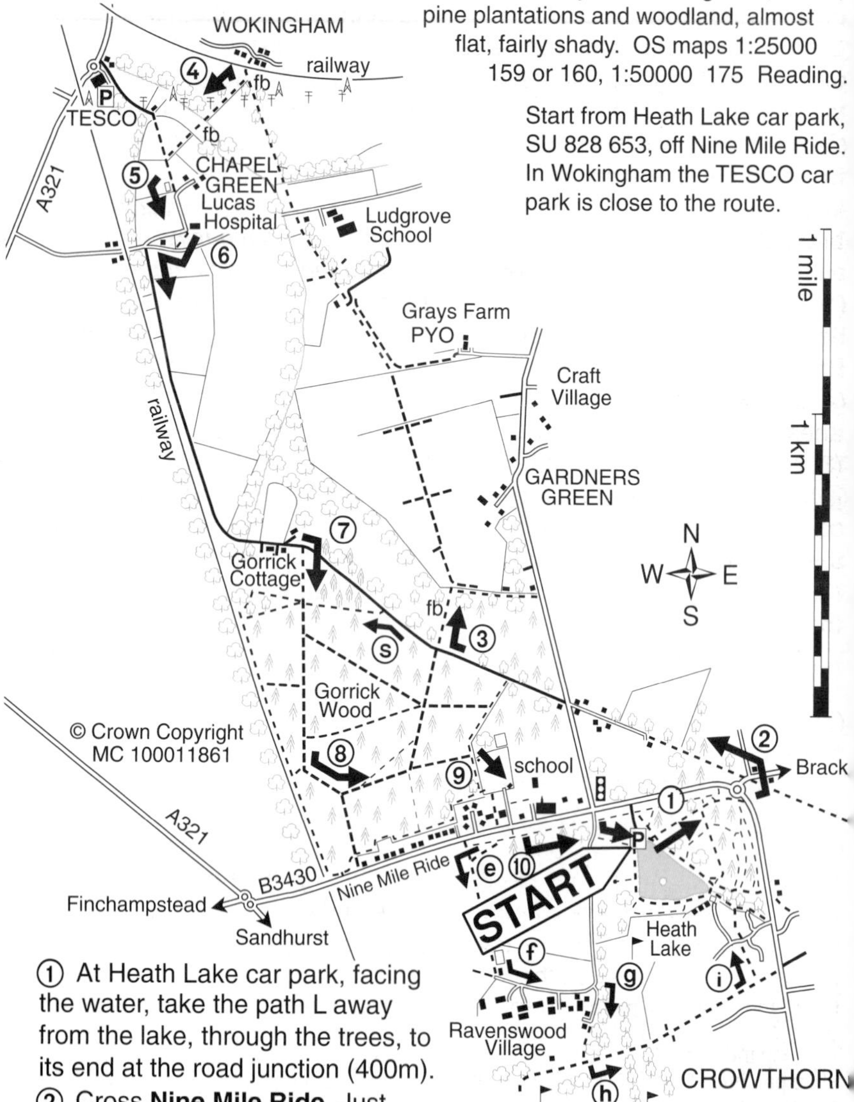

① At Heath Lake car park, facing the water, take the path L away from the lake, through the trees, to its end at the road junction (400m).

② Cross **Nine Mile Ride**. Just beyond the roundabout (50m) take the track back L (400m). Continue on the tarmac lane (300m), across the road and on the track to the next track junction (450m).

ⓢ *Short cut of 2¼ km/1½miles: Stay on the track ahead (600m) and turn L on the second side path just before signs of habitation. →⑦*

③ Turn R along the side path in the wood (200m). Just after a footbridge enter the field ahead and continue on farm tracks over the fruit fields (800m). In the last fruit field the footpath continues at the L edge (200m). Go on between the trees and small fields to the drive of Ludgrove School (300m). Cross and carry on between fields up to the **railway** line (Staines-Wokingham) (500m).

④ Don't cross the footbridge but take the footpath back L. Continue in the same direction over the brook (200m) and up to the horse track between paddocks (150m).

⑤ Go L on the horse track (80m) and continue on the lane to Lucas Hospital L (150m).

⑥ At the bend pass into the field ahead and cross diagonally R (80m). Turn R on the drive to the junction (100m) then turn L on the track. Continue between fields and the **railway** (Reading-Guildford) (950m). Stay on the track round the L curve (250m) past Gorrick Cottage R and turn R at the next side path (70m).

⑦ Follow the path through the forest (150m) and continue ahead on the wide forest track. Disregard side tracks and paths (600m).

⑧ Carry on round the L bend (150m) but when the track bends R towards the road, fork L on the side track (250m). When the track bends ½L stay ahead on the lesser track to the cross path (250m).

⑨ Find the path ½R into the cricket field (20m) and cross to the gate R of the pavilion (120m). Walk out to the road (100m) and cross to the path in the wood (40m).

ⓔ *Extension of 2 km km/1¼ mile: Turn R on the path parallel with the road (200m). At the end turn L on the path through the wood (100m). At the cross path bear R over the stream (20m) and carry on to the end (400m).*

ⓕ *Go L along the main drive of Ravenswood Village until it bends L beside the trees (350m).*

ⓖ *Go R on the side drive. When it bends to the buildings keep on along the footpath to the golf course boundary path (250m).*

ⓗ *Turn L along the public footpath straight across the fairways to the edge of the golf course (200m) then on under the trees between houses. Disregard the first side paths but watch out for the long straight side path L between back gardens (450m).*

ⓘ *Follow it to the road (120m). Slightly R carry on as before to the end of the housing estate (100m). Bear L along the edge of the wood to the footbridge R and Heath Lake (80m). Walk round the lake to the car park clockwise (500m) or over the bridge & anticlockwise (300m).*

⑩ Turn L and follow the path parallel with the road, under trees to the Ravenswood Drive (300m).

⑪ Just along the drive R (50m), find the narrow path on the other side through the trees to Heath Lake and car park (150m).

Ravenswood Village is a charitable home for the care and education of the mentally handicapped. It was set up in 1953 on the site of the house of the Ravenswood family and is now a division of the larger Norwood Trust. There are about 200 residents, 75% Jewish. Historically the Ravenswood estate corresponds to Bigshott Walk of the Easthampstead bailiwick of Windsor Great Forest and was called Bigshott Rayles after the Forest was enclosed and sold. It acquired the new name some time before 1860.

6 Around Finchampstead

About 8½ km/5 miles; over fields, undulating, several stiles. Avoid in wet winters. OS maps 1:25000 159 Reading, 1:50000 175 or 186.

Start from the car park or roadside at Finchampstead Church, SU 792 638, or from California Country Park, SU 785 649 (payment at weekends).

The Greyhound ☎ 0118 973 2305 ***The Queen's Oak*** ☎ 0118 973 4855

Linking wallks
7✻ 27✻ 29☆ 30☆

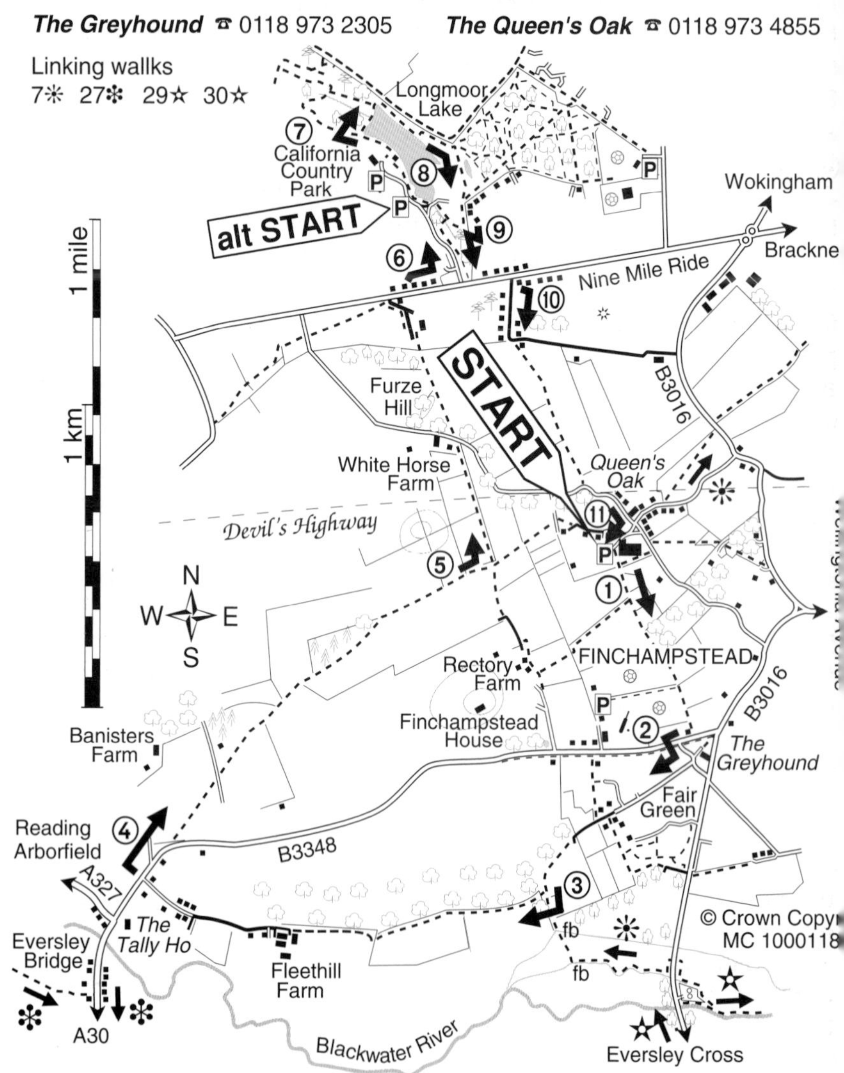

✻ ① At **Finchampstead Church** identify the brickwork of the tower and the nearby brick shed then go down the path behind the church, off the mound, into the trees. Keep on to the road (700m).

② At the road go down R (60m) and L into Longwater Lane to the first junction (80m). This is Fair Green. (The back entrance to the ***Greyhound*** is L 50m.) Turn R down the branch Longwater Lane

(350m). ✦ When the tarmac ends continue on a track (150m). When it bends L, stay ahead on the path outside the field (200m). ☆

③ Just round the end of the field (50m) take the side path R into the field. Stay at the R edge of the fields next to the wood to Fleethill Farm (900m) then ahead on track and drive to the road (550m). ❇

④ Walk up the road R (100m). Just over the crest of the hill (50m) turn L along the path in the field (300m). Cross a tarmac drive and continue in the same line along a fenced footpath over several fields past the house on the hill (far R) to a 4-way path junction (1150m).

⑤ Enter the field L and follow the R edge to the lane at White Horse Farm (400m). Cross and carry on between fields (400m) then follow the drive to the main road, **Nine Mile Ride** (150m).

⑥ Cross to the pavement and go R (250m) then L on the drive to **California** Country Park (250m).

⑦ From the first car park make your way to Longmoor Lake then follow the bank round the end to the far corner (400m) and back on the other side (200m).

⑧ Keep to the tarmac path which bends L away from the water's edge to the end of the field (100m), then R below the wooded slope. Continue to the boundary and R of the houses into the trees (200m).

⑨ Go round the U-bend in the path (50m) then cross the footbridge L (20m). Take the path L parallel with the drive, out of the wood and bear L over the grass to the road (250m). Walk along the pavement L (150m).

⑩ Cross the road and walk along Warren Lane (200m). Just round the bend go R on the path between fields (500m). The **Devil's Highway** passes under the top end. Walk up the lane L to the ***Queen's Oak*** crossroads (200m).

⑪ Ascend to the church on the mound, via the road or through the churchyard (100m).

English bond, alternate courses of stretchers and headers, was the first fixed pattern used in all-brick walls. It was in the 16th century that bricks came into use and they were thinner.

Flemish bond - alternating stretchers and headers in each course - appears first in 1631 in Dutch House, Kew, but took a century to become widely used - sometimes with burnt end headers. It soon went out of general use but is still applied in decorative brickwork.

It gave way to courses with two, three or more stretchers between headers - common throughout the 19th century.

Stretcher bond became the norm for cavity walls early in the 20th century for headers could not bridge the gap.

7 Finchampstead and the Blackwater River

About 9 km/ 5½ miles; over fields, undulating. Avoid before summer because of muddy bridleways. OS maps 1:25000 159 Reading, 1:50000 175 Reading.

Start from Finchampstead Church parking in the car park, SU 792 638, or at the roadside. Alternatively start from Colebrook Lake car park, SU 805 628. There is verge parking on Finchampstead Ridges, SU 809 634.

Linking walks 6✳ 8❖ 29★ 30★

The Queen's Oak
☎ 0118 973 4855

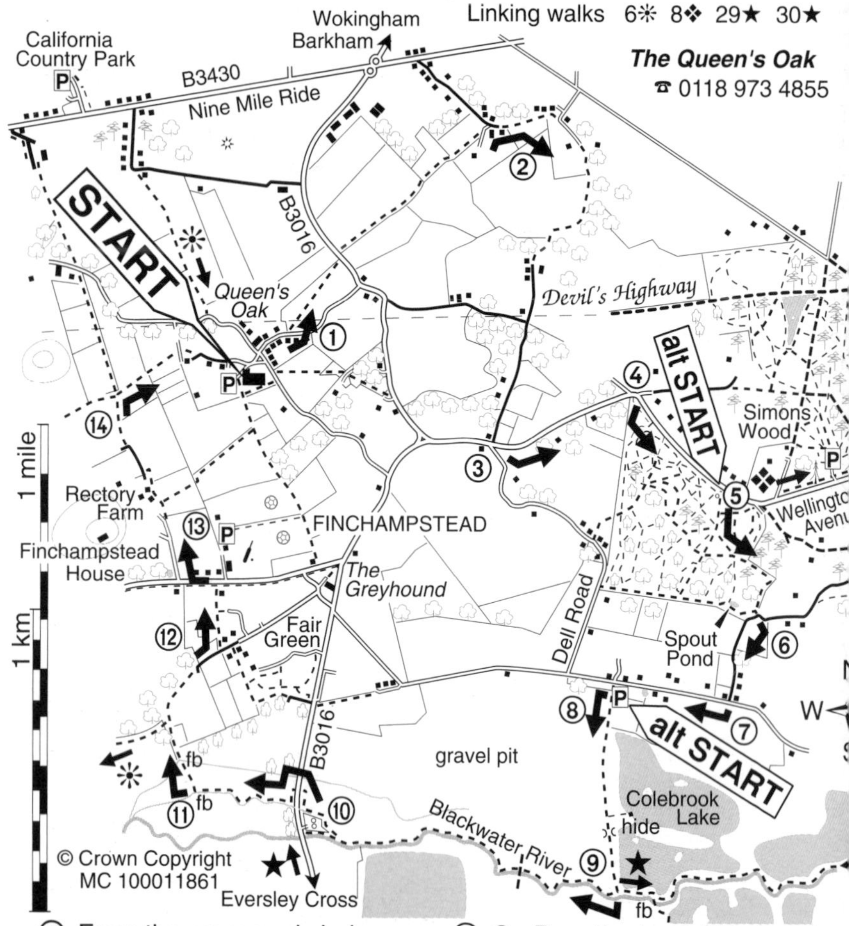

① From the crossroads below **Finchampstead Church** take the road past the front of the ***Queen's Oak*** (200m). After the last house L enter the field L and make for the bottom L corner (250m). Cross the road slightly L and continue up the R edge of the field on the other side. Stay ahead between fields to the track with houses (700m).

② Go R on the track (50m) and continue on the path down to the tarmac drive (200m). Go R (120m). At the end of the tarmac continue on the bridleway under trees and up round the edge of a field to the vehicle track and houses on top (450m). Stay ahead past a side track (near the **Devil's Highway**) (250m) to the road (400m).

③ Cross the road and go L along it; it soon has a verge (500m).

④ On the R bend take the path R into the trees of **Finchampstead Ridges** and make your way along the hillside parallel with the road, within 50m of it, to the National Trust stone (500m).

⑤ At the stone follow the main path away from the road to the edge of the ridge (150m) and descend the widest path to the first cross path below (100m). Go L on the cross path along the hillside (200m) and down round the boundary to the gateway (100m).❖

⑥ Join the vehicle track, outside the gateway, and descend R past houses to the road (400m).

⑦ Walk along the road R to the side path and car park L (400m).

⑧ Take the path from the car park beside **Colebrook Lake**, past the side path to the bird hide (450m) and on to the Blackwater **River** (250m). ★❊

⑨ Turn R and follow the path along the bank of the winding river almost to the next road (1100m).

⑩ At the little sewage works take the side path R to the road (250m). Cross into the field opposite and go L beside the road (70m) then R away from the road. Stay at the L edge to the end of the field (350m).

⑪ Cross the footbridge and turn R between the fields. Go on under trees, past a side path L (250m), ❊ and round R almost to the road and houses of Fair Green (300m).

⑫ Go L on the footpath outside the end of the last field, over a rise and down to the road (200m).

⑬ Walk along the pavement L to the drive of Rectory Farrn and Finchamstead House opposite (150m). Go along the drive (200m). Just before Rectory Farm take the footpath skirting R of the buildings (200m), then continue up between fields to the 4-way path junction on top (300m).

⑭ Turn R on the footpath between fields (250m). Cross the tarmac drive and continue up ahead under trees (70m). On top continue on the track then road to the cross-roads below the church (250m).

The **Devil's Highway** was the Roman road from London to *Calleva Atrebatum*, Silchester. It crosses the routes of many walks in this book, often under tracks and roads that are still in use. At Finchampstead it passes beneath the fields just north of the church and was the basis for the suggestion that the church mound had Roman significance. In the parish it changes width from 28' to 17' and contains iron slag and pottery shards of 130-140 AD. A Roman mile stone turned up by a ploughman in 1841 stands in the garden of Banister's.

The first comprehensive survey was made in 1836 by Sandhurst students tracing the road westwards from the Thames at *Pontes*, Staines. It forms parts of the county boundary of Berkshire with Hampshire and Surrey, evidence that it was in use when the counties were delineated. Parish boundaries suggests it issued out of Newgate on the line of Oxford Street. It is the only known great west road from London, perhaps because of difficult forest terrain, and *Calleva Atrebatum* was the hub of all the other Roman western arterial routes. Copies of a Roman gazetteer have survived with lists of distances from main centres of the empire. Places on this road are listed in Iters VII & XV. The document is known as the *Antonine Itineraries* and thought to be a route planner for itinerant civil servants. *Roman Roads in Britain* Ivan D Margary Ed 3 1973 John Baker 550pp

8 Colebrook Lake and Wellingtonia Avenue

About 6½ km/4 miles with an extension of 3 km/2 miles and a short cut of 1 km/¾ mile. Good for birds, summer and winter; one short steep hill. OS maps 1:25000 159 Reading or 160 Windsor, 1:50000 175 Reading.

Start at Horseshoe Lake car park, SU 820 620, near the watersports centre or Simons Wood car park SU 813 635 halfway along Wellingtonia Avenue. The Ambarrow car park, SU 824 626, is on the extension.

Linking walks 7❖ 29✿ 30✻

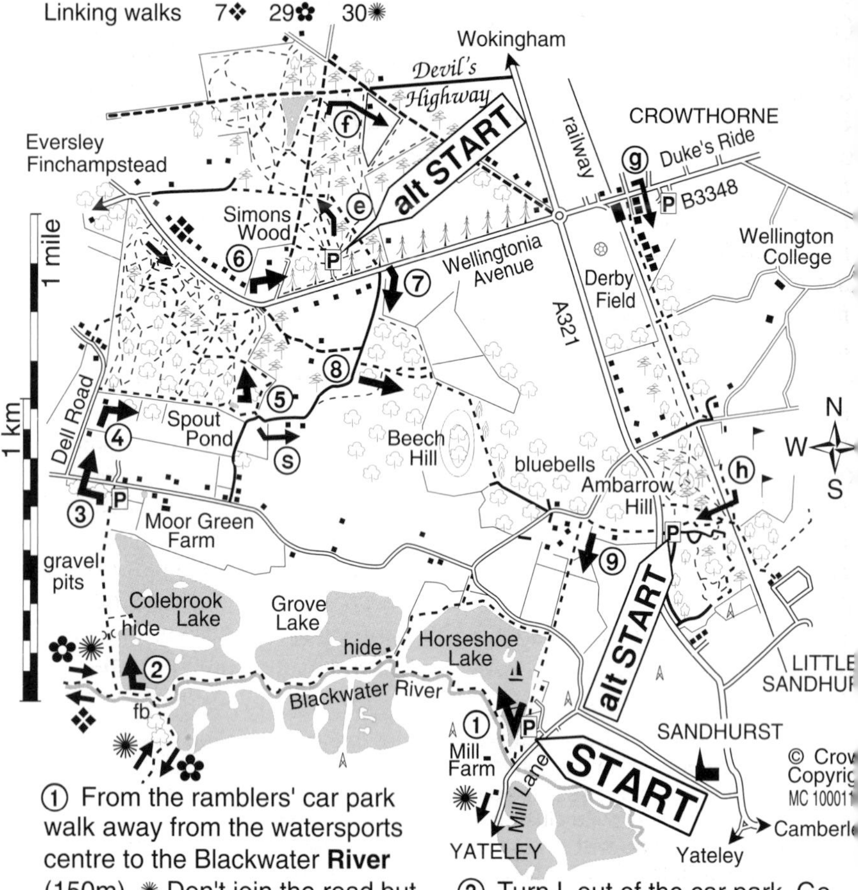

① From the ramblers' car park walk away from the watersports centre to the Blackwater **River** (150m). ✻ Don't join the road but go R along the winding river bank past Horseshoe Lake, a side path R at the hide (600m) and Grove Lake R to the footbridge (900m). ✿

② Carry on by the river to the end of Colebrook Lake (100m) ❖ then turn R along the path across the end of the lake, past another hide, to the car park (700m).

③ Turn L out of the car park. Go along the lane (200m) and up the 1st R, Dell Road to the track, R, after the 2nd house (350m).

④ Go through the wood to Spout Pond L (500m).

ⓢ *Short cut missing Wellingtonia Avenue: Go up to the end of the path after the pond (50m) and join the vehicle track. Follow the track up L to houses then down and up again, disregarding small divergent paths R (600m).* ➧⑧

⑤ At the pond, turn L up the hillside. At the wide cross path take one of the steep paths up to the road on **Finchampstead Ridges** at the R end of the heath (450m).

⑥ Cross and turn R (100m) then. follow the path, L behind the trees, along Wellingtonia Avenue to Simons Wood car park (300m).

ⓔ *Extension of 3 km/2 miles: At the end of the car park, opposite the road entrance, take the level middle path through the wood to the fork (100m) then bear L down to the junction of path and track at a boundary mound (100m). Walk down the track R (100m), L on the side path to the pool (100m) and R around the edge (200m).*

ⓕ *At the end of the lake go R on the rising track* (**Devil's Highway**), *(150m) and R again on the oblique cross track to the road junction (750m). Cross and continue beside the road to* **Crowthorne** *(250m).*

ⓖ *Take the first side path R after the bridge and continue beside the (Reading-Guildford)* **railway**, *past the sports field footbridge (400m) to the next bridge (400m). Follow the drive L from the bridge (40m) and turn R along the path between fields watching out for the gate R just after the wood starts (400m).*

ⓗ *Cross the lines and fork L on the path away from the railway to* **Ambarrow** *car park (250m).*

ⓘ *Cross the road and take the footpath between gardens and field (250m). At the lane join the next footpath L (10m).* ➧⑨

⑦ Continue down Wellingtonia Avenue to the boundary track of Simons Wood (100m). Cross the road and go up the track past a side track R (330m) and on (40m).

⑧ At the very top take the path into the wood along the ridge and drop off the end (250m). Descend between fields and through the bluebell wood to the lane (650m). Walk up the lane L to the first footpath R on the bend (100m).

⑨ Go down the R edge of the fields (350m), over the road and on, L of the lake, past the water sports hut, to the car park (300m).

Wellingtonia, the California Big Tree, *Sequoiadendron gigantea* (formerly Sequoia gigantea), has scale leaves. The twigs dangle like clusters of rat tails. The bark is soft (try thumping it) and resists fire. The species is native to the western slopes of the Sierra Navada, California.

The two Sequoias are the tallest trees in the world, up to 110m tall. Both are grown in British parks and gardens .

California Redwood, *Sequoia sempervirens*, has twigs that are yew-like though with stiffer pointed leaves, grey beneath. It is native to the sea-board of North California.

x1

9 Crowthorne, Broadmoor and Cæsar's Camp

About 9 km/5½ miles; extended version 2 km/1¼ miles longer. Many variants possible; mainly pine woods; short steep hills; dry under foot. OS maps 1:25000 160 Windsor, 1:50000 175 Reading.

Start from the parking bays near Crowthorne Library, SU 841 637. Wildmoor Heath car park is close to the route, SU 838 630.

Linking walks 10❖ 11★ 1✻

The Iron Duke
☎ 01344 772568

The Crowthorne Inn
☎ 01344 775886

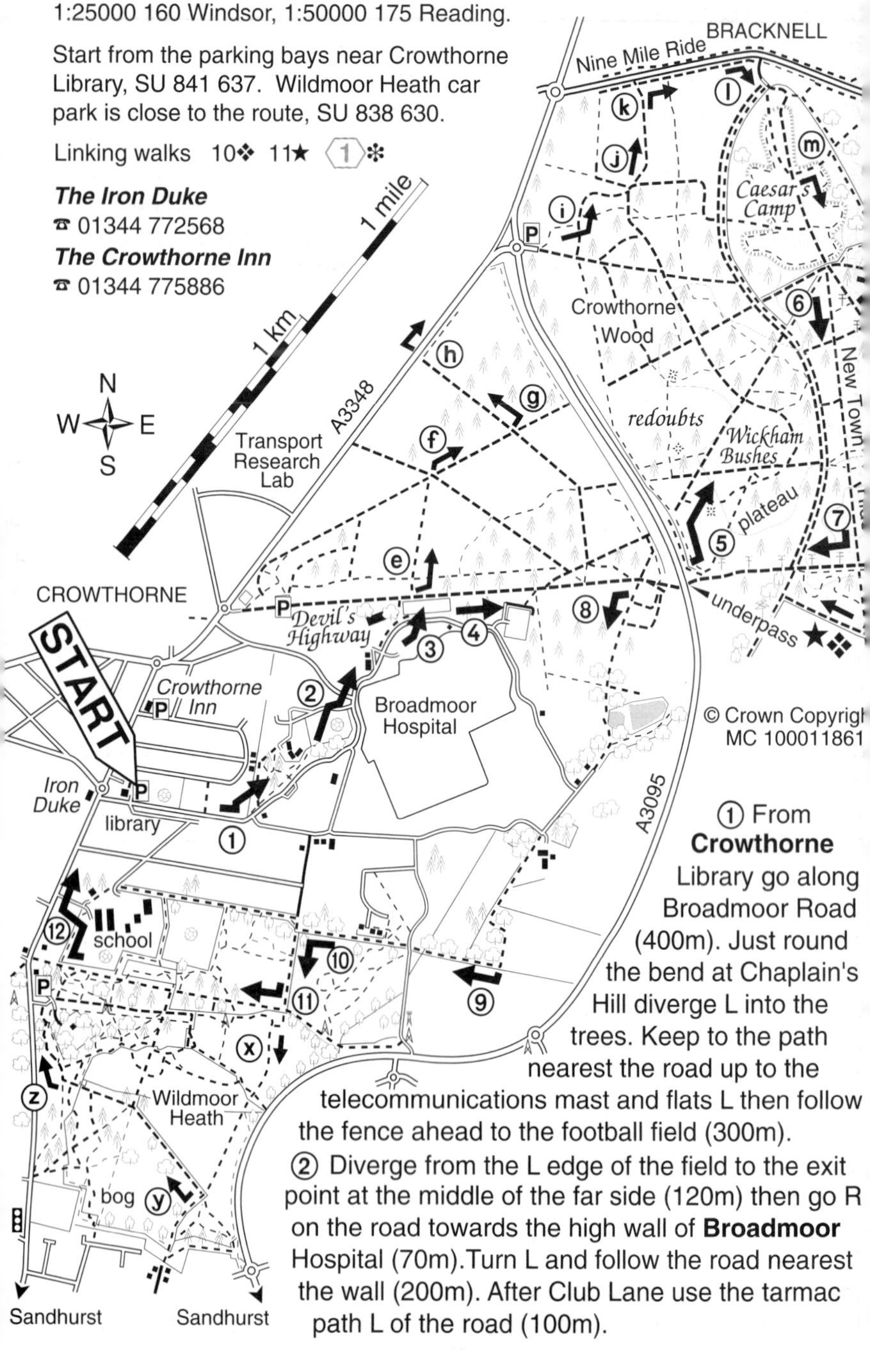

① From **Crowthorne** Library go along Broadmoor Road (400m). Just round the bend at Chaplain's Hill diverge L into the trees. Keep to the path nearest the road up to the telecommunications mast and flats L then follow the fence ahead to the football field (300m).

② Diverge from the L edge of the field to the exit point at the middle of the far side (120m) then go R on the road towards the high wall of **Broadmoor** Hospital (70m). Turn L and follow the road nearest the wall (200m). After Club Lane use the tarmac path L of the road (100m).

③ Just over the brow of the hill, at the end of the clubhouse L, take the side path down L in the trees beside the car park to the **Devil's Highway** track (100m) and turn R.

ⓔ *Extended version: Almost immediately (30m) take the path L to the forestry track (400m).*

ⓕ *Turn R over the track junction. Go on to the next crossing (400m).*

ⓖ *Turn L to the road (450m).*

ⓗ *Cross to the pavement and go R (but if you are nimble follow the forestry track beside the road to the end then cross the ditch to the road). When the road splits (400m) join the R verge of the R road and go on to the roundabout. Cross into the side road (150m).*

ⓘ *At Crowthorne Wood parking area follow the first path L from the forest track (250m). Go L at the next track, round a R curve to join a major track on the bend (250m).*

ⓙ *Bear L on the other side track down to the end (350m).*

ⓚ *Turn R on the track near the road* (**Nine Mile Ride**) *up to the cross track from the road (450m).*

ⓛ *Follow the track away from the road round L & R bends (100m). Go through the fence and up to the* **plateau** *then on the level through* **Cæsar's Camp** *(300m).*

ⓜ *Just after the converging path joins, turn L on the footpath out to the ramparts (70m) and follow them round R to the vehicle gate through the fence (450m).* ➧⑥

④ Stay on the undulating track and pass under the road (900m).

⑤ After the underpass (50m), turn L on the path between fences near the road (250m). At the end of the fenced section turn R up the wide path. Notice the **redoubts**. Stay ahead over two cross tracks to the double cross track (750m) and up between fences to the gateway of the **Cæsar's Camp** enclosure (250m). Inside the fence go along a side path R or L (50m) to see the ramparts then return (or go right round & back to the gate (950m).)

⑥ Emerging from the gateway, ❖❈ disregard tracks R & ahead and take the level one between. Stay ahead to the major cross track with power lines (Devil's Highway) at the edge of the plateau (1000m).★

⑦ Go R on the track and down under the road (600m).

⑧ After the underpass, at the end of the cutting (100m), take the downhill side path to Butter Bottom Ponds (400m). Stay ahead up to the house (100m), along the road to the T-junction (300m) and down the path between woods and fields (300m). In the wood, after the fields (40m), the path bends L up a slope (50m) then R along the edge of the wood (150m).

⑨ At the end of the wood take the path R along the boundary under trees (300m) over the lane and on to a T-junction of paths (400m).

⑩ Go L along the fence down to the corner (250m).

ⓧⓨⓩ *Extension of 900m on map.*

⑪ Turn R along the main path under the trees to the end of the school fields R (800m). If making for **Wildmoor Heath** car park turn L through the trees (150m). If not:-

⑫ Go up the L edge of the field (200m), out L to the main road (100m) then along the pavement R to the ***Iron Duke*** (400m). Turn R for the library parking area (100m).

10 Swinley Forest and Cæsar's Camp

About 7 km/4½ miles with an extension of 1 km/½ mile; many extensions and short cuts can be devised; mainly through pine woods; short steep hills; dry under foot. OS maps 1:25000 160 Windsor, 1:50000 175 Reading.

Start from The Look Out car park, SU 877 661, on the B3430. The Crowthorne Wood car park on the A3095, SU 854 655, is near the extension.

Linking walks 9❖ 11✷ 12✧ ⟨2⟩✪

The Look Out cafe ☎ 01344 868222.

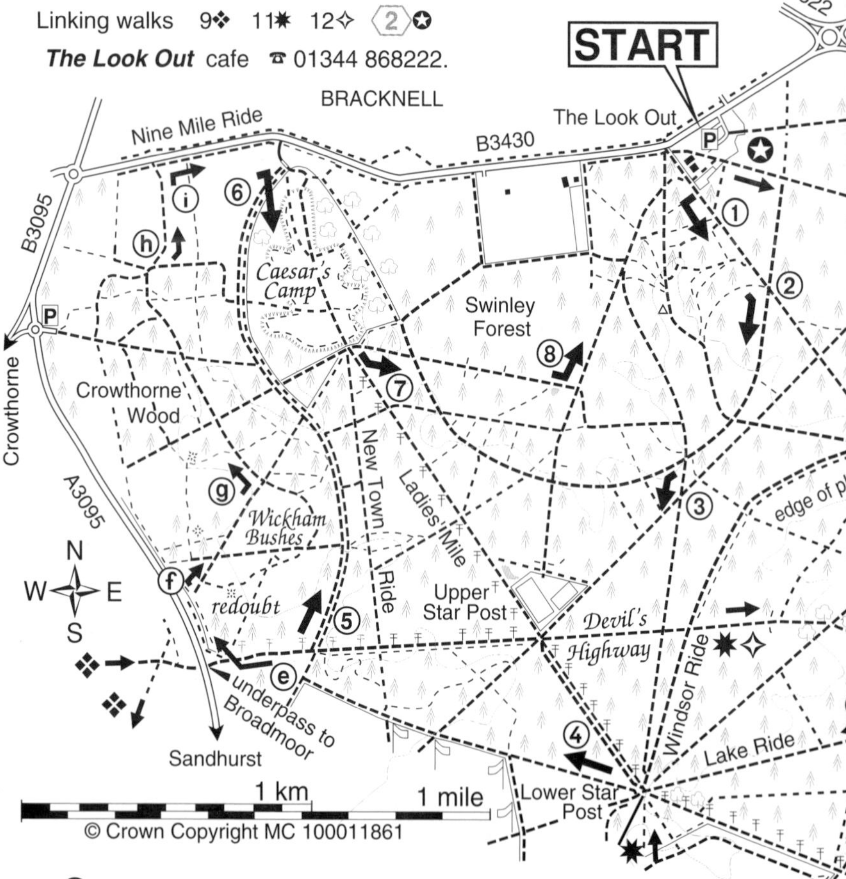

✪① From the **Look Out** car park follow the path L of the buildings (100m). Outside the fence, go L on the wide path over a little rise (150m) and on (300m).

② Just after the next rise, turn R up the oblique cross track onto the **plateau**. Disregard the 1st cross track (450m) and go on to the next track junction where there is a steep embankment (200m).

③ Bear L on the straight track. Cross an oblique track (150m) and a straight track (**Devil's Highway**)(450m)✧✷ and continue to Lower Star Post, where numerous tracks meet (600m).

④ Turn R on the track after the one with the power cables. At the ranges (450m) continue beside the fence to the end (750m) then up R to the track with power lines (80m).

ⓔ *Extension of 1 km/½ mile: Go L down the wide track (300m).* ❖ *50m before the underpass bear R on the path between fences near the road (250m).*

ⓕ *At the end of the fenced section turn R up the wide path. Disregard the oblique sloping cross track (200m) but turn L at the curving track on the plateau (300m).*

ⓖ *Stay ahead over the 1st cross track (300m) and the 2nd (250m) and down the slope to the bend with side tracks (300m).*

ⓗ *Just round the bend branch L on the track in the original direction down to the road (350m).*

ⓘ *Turn R on the track near the road and stay on it up to the cross track from the road (450m), then go R up to the fence around Cæsar's Camp (100m).* ➧⑥

⑤ Continue ahead on the track L of the boundary mound. It curves and undulates past several side tracks and eventually descends beside the fence of Cæsar's Camp (visible above) to a track from the road (1900m). Turn back R.

⑥ Go up the steep footpath to the flat top (80m). Either stay ahead through the middle of **Cæsar's Camp** (500m) or diverge R round the ramparts (disregard the sloping cross path) (850m). Exit at the gate to the level track junction.

⑦ Take the L track which soon curves away from the fence. Disregard the cross track just off the **plateau** and keep on to the next major cross track (800m).

⑧ Turn L up over a rise (150m). Stay ahead on this track eventually curving R to the Look Out (700m).

The **Bagshot Sands** (in the original sense) are a mound in the middle of the London Basin, on which stands Camberley. They underlie all the walks in this book though the northern and western walks stray onto the London Clay.

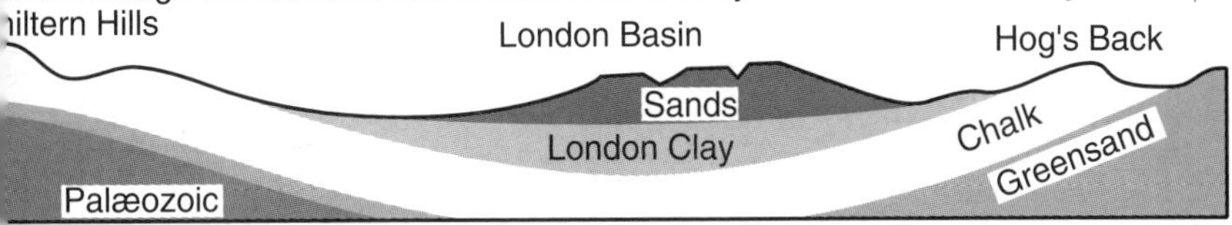

iltern Hills
London Basin
Hog's Back
Sands
London Clay
Chalk
Greensand
Palæozoic

The Sands make up a geological stratum 250 feet thick but are not lithified - turned to rock. The first description of them was read to the Geological Sociey of London by Henry Warburton in 1821 and the name stuck. The Middle and Upper layers became the Bracklesham and Barton Sands when correlated with outcrops elsewhere and *Bagshot* is retained only for the lowest division. The whole thickness is now called the Tertiary Sands or the Bagshot Series.

These Sands stretch to the heaths of Dorset and to the Ypres and Paris Basins. Fifty million years ago they were beaches in a large estuary where the earth's crust was slowly sinking. Beach sand is coarse and does not lie in level layers; it grinds sea shells away. The Bagshot and Bracklesham Sands seen in fresh cuttings show current bedding and worm burrows but very few other fossils.

At thickest, the Bagshot Beds are 130'. The Bracklesham Beds, which make up most of the land surface, are 70' thick. Within them are sporadic clay beds which make the sand above boggy and were dug for brick, tile and pot making, commemorated by names like *Pottery Lane*. The full thickness of the Barton Sands is unknown; only 50' remain in the tops of Ash Ranges, Bagshot Heath, Chobham Ridges and Yateley Common. It is they which yield the heathstone boulders which are called sarsens when left exposed by erosion,

11 Barossa Common and the Devil's Highway

About 7 km/4¼ miles; a cut 2 km/1¼ mile and an extension of 1 km/¾ mile may be used together; on heath. You may find yourself in the middle of a noisy army exercise! OS maps 1:25000 160 Windsor, 1:50000 175 Reading.

Park near the bend at the north end of the road, Kings Ride, SU 875 621.

Linking walks 9★ 10✸ 12✹ ⟨1⟩☆ ⟨2⟩❊

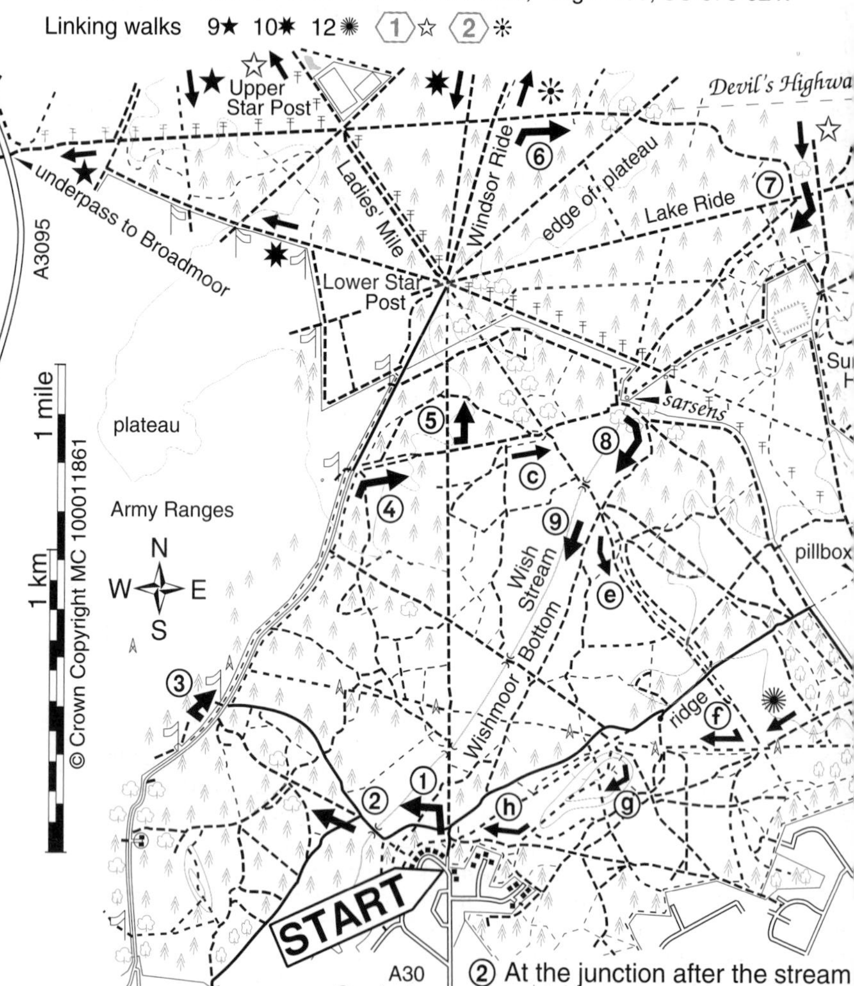

① From the Kings Ride road bend descend the tarmac drive then the track into **Barossa Common** (120m). Disregard the first side tracks but turn L on the hard track at the major junction. Stay on this track round L and R bends and over the **Wish Stream** (250m).

② At the junction after the stream (50m), take the uphill track in the angle between the hard tracks. Stay ahead to the boundary road and fence on the **plateau** (550m).

③ Turn R. Walk on the tarmac or one of the paths beside it (200m). After the power cables keep on to the double side track R, opposite a gate in the fence (800m).

④ Bear R on the double track. After a dip ascend to the cross-roads on the rise (300m).

ⓒ *Cut of 2 km/1¼ mile: Stay on the same track ahead to the bottom of the valley (600m) then turn R outside the fence. ➔⑧*

⑤ Turn onto the track L and keep on, over a wide track to Lower Star Point where numerous tracks meet (550m). ★☆✸ Continue ahead on Windsor Ride, the main track R of the one with power lines (600m). ⁂

⑥ Turn R at the long straight cross track (**Devil's Highway**). Continue on the level (300m) then drop to an oblique cross track (200m). Go on ahead down round curves LRLR to end at a straight track (600m). ✸

⑦ Cross the straight track and turn R up the diverging side track. Pass over the rise and down to the cross track at power lines (750m). Stay ahead, L of the fence, to the next corner (150m), then pass out through the opening and L.

⑧ See the **Wishmoor Stone** at opening in the fence. Cross the cart bridge over the **Wish** Stream to the 3-way fork (80m) and take the R track round a R bend to the next cross track (400m).

ⓔ *Extension of 1 km/¾ mile: There are three adjacent tracks L. Take the 3rd one up the valleyside to the hard track on the ridge (650m). Go straight down the other side to the power lines (300m).*

ⓕ *Turn R along one of the paths following the power lines past the next pylon (400m).*

ⓖ *On the rise after the pylon (100m), turn L up Saddleback Hill (70m). Stay on the ridge to the end (350m) and drop off to the wide path across the foot (50m).*

ⓗ *Turn R down to the hard track (300m) then up L to the starting point (100m).*

⑨ Stay ahead on the track along Wishmoor Bottom, over a cross track (600m), under power cables (150m) to the end (250m). Follow the hard track down R (150m) and turn L up between the houses to the starting point (120m).

The A30 runs to Land's End. It follows the old road from London which forked at Basingstoke to Winchester and Salisbury - successor to the Roman road from which it diverged after the Thames and which branched at Silchester.

From Egham to Hartley Wintney, the old road cut up the heath on the Tertiary Sands though not exactly on the present line. It would have been a multiplicity of rutted tracks, not a paved way of Roman type. Road renaissance came with the Turnpike Acts. The heath road was turnpiked from Hounslow to the Basing-stone (Bagshot boundary at the *Jolly Farmer*) by an Act of 1728 and from there to Hertfordbridge Hill (*White Lion*, Hartley Wintney) by an Act of 1857.

Medieval roads were the responsibility of Lords of the Manor. When manors became fragmented by land sales, parishes were charged with the task (1555). Parishes overwhelmed by the Great North Road on their clay soils obtained a Highways Act in 1663 enabling them to collect tolls, Wadesmill having first the gate. Earlier turnstiles with pikes to prevent horses passing provided the name.

Turnpike roads became trusts which erected gates and employed toll keepers. They lacked technology but had the ruts filled, instigated new roads on better routes and initiated legislation. Many A-roads are new roads of that period. Later the trusts would appoint engineers: Jack Metcalf, Thomas Telford, John Loudon McAdam, and road building technology was re-born.

12 Bagshot Heath

About 8 km/5¼ miles; this is an introduction to some of main landmarks. Pine woods and open heath; short steep hills; dry under foot; very flinty in places; bluebells in season. OS maps 1:25000 160 Windsor, 1:50000 175 Reading.

Start from near Bagshot Church, SU 905 632. Park near the start of the gravel track a little way into Vicarage Road. No pub but places for picnics.

Linking walks 10✧ 11✺ 13✾ ⟨1⟩✦ ⟨2⟩✻

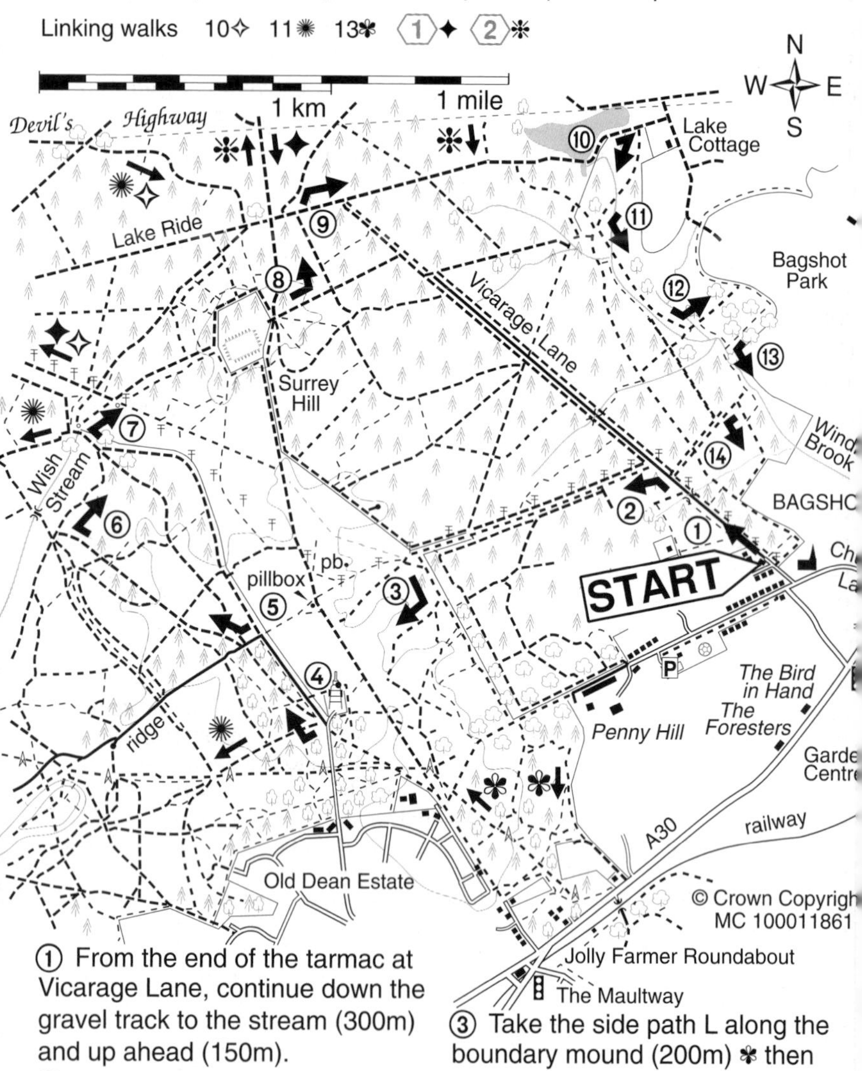

① From the end of the tarmac at Vicarage Lane, continue down the gravel track to the stream (300m) and up ahead (150m).

② Turn L on the side path between fences (where power lines cross). Stay on this path, parallel with forest tracks, to the end corner of the boundary mound L (850m).

③ Take the side path L along the boundary mound (200m) ✾ then diverge R up the valley towards the **telecommunications tower**. Make your way over the **plateau** to the foot of the tower and around it L to the gate at the road (500m).

④ With your back to the gate take the straight hard track R, diverging from the end of the road (350m) or the small path L of it.

⑤ At the major side track go L to the two side tracks R (70m).✷ Take the second one across the plateau and down to the T-junction near the bottom of the valley (750m).

⑥ Go R on the main track and stay on it round L bends and over the Wish Stream (450m). ✧✦

⑦ Before the corner, pass through the fence at the **Wishmoor** Stone and take the track back R. Near the top of **Surrey Hill** skirt L round the reservoir fence (800m).

⑧ Leave the plateau hilltop via the track which comes straight from the gate of the reservoir (200m). At the first cross track go L to the long straight track, Lake Ride (300m). ✻

⑨ Follow Lake Ride gently down to Rapley Lake (900m). Cross the bridge and carry on (250m).

⑩ Near the end of the track turn off R beside a fence and follow the path (400m).

⑪ At the next 4-way junction turn down L, cross a culvert and carry on near the stream (500m).

⑫ At the end, take the path L up to the boundary of **Bagshot Park** (250m). Go R along the fence under the trees (150m) then down R into the bluebell wood (200m).

⑬ After the culvert, go L beside the **Windle** Brook (200m) then turn R towards the clearing (50m).

⑭ Before the clearing, go L along the side path to the boundary (250m) then keep to the boundary path R (200m) then L (300m) then R to Vicarage Road (200m).

Bagshot Heath Highwaymen:

Bagshot Heath in the 18th century was a large part of the uninhabited country stretching from the Thames, through Bagshot to Hartley Wintney. The volume of traffic on the great west road (A30) in this wild country made it a profitable work-place for highwaymen, several of whom based themselves nearby.

William Davis, 1627-90, the Golden Farmer, was born at Wrexham. At Bagshot he farmed successfully for 40 years, a pillar of the community with 18 children, concealing his "other job" by operating at night and during travels. He retired to a corn chandler's shop in London in 1685 but came out of retirement and was shot by a coach passenger. It is known he was taken to the *Kings Arms* in Bagshot but there is no record of a trial. Ultimately he was taken at Southwark, executed at Tyburn (Fleet Street) and gibbetted on Bagshot Heath opposite his house. The original pub of the same name may have been his house. Rocque's map of Surrey of 1770 shows the *Golden Farmer* on the north side of the major road at the Maultway junction and in the position of the *Jolly Farmer* (as was) but it may have been on the other side originally. It became *Jolly* in 1823.

The Golden Farmer - Inn and Highwayman George Poulter 1973 18pp

Claude Duval had a house in Lightwater Lane. He came over from Normandy in the service of travellers and was a page to the Duke of Richmond before taking to the road. Stories of chivalrous highwaymen appear to emanate from him. He retired but came out of retirement and was captured in London. Several well-born ladies petitioned on his behalf and Mr Justice Morgan threatened to resign if he was reprieved. He was executed in 1670.

Parson Darby was a curate and resident of Yateley. He shot dead a Royal Mail coach driver in 1835 at the Wooden House tavern, Pinetree Hill, and was subsequently gibbetted there. It is said Darby Green takes its name from him.

13 High Curley and Lightwater Country Park

About 8½ km/5¼ miles with an extension of 1 km/¾ mile to the Heatherside Wellingtonias; heath with long views; short steep slopes, half shady. Part of the route crosses army land with vehicle test tracks. Step into the trees if vehicles approach. OS maps 1:25000 160 Windsor, 1:50000 186 or 175.

Start at the car park beside the Maultway 350m from Jolly Farmer roundabout, SU 900 617, or park in Lightwater Country Park, SU 917 619. On the extension use the Cumberland Road car park, SU 905 598.

Linking walks 12✾ 14★ 1❄

The Wheatsheaf ☎ 01276 28744

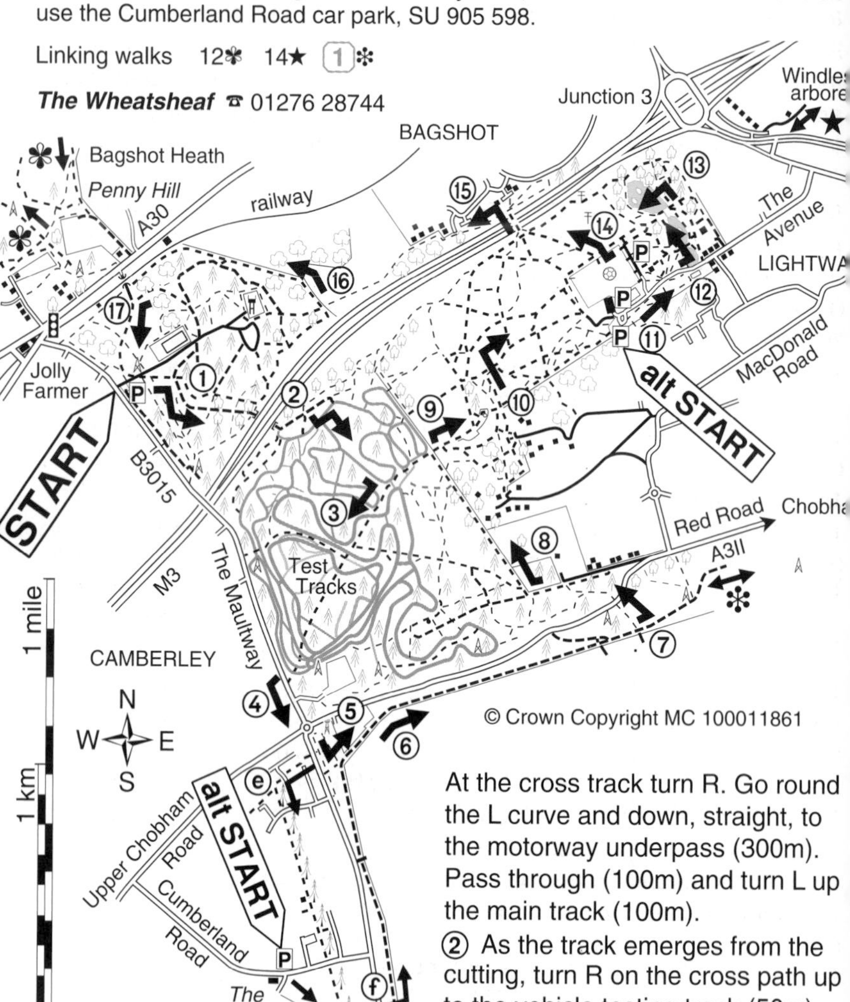

① At the Maultway car park, take the main track away from the road (100m). Under the power cables diverge on the side track R (120m). At the cross track turn R. Go round the L curve and down, straight, to the motorway underpass (300m). Pass through (100m) and turn L up the main track (100m).

② As the track emerges from the cutting, turn R on the cross path up to the vehicle testing track (50m). Follow it down L (80m) then turn R on the uphill side track. Stay ahead on this track to the top of **High Curley** (300m). Where the track curves L to descend, step out on to the ridge path.

③ Turn R and follow the ridge path between and across tracks to the road (Maultway) at the edge of **Camberley** (750m).

④ Go L on the pavement to the roundabout (150m) and ahead.

ⓔ *Extension of 1 km/¾ mile via the Heatherside Wellingtonias: After the roundabout (100m), take the path R between houses and across a road to the avenue of Wellingtonias (150m). Walk along the path beneath the trees to Cumberland Road (600m). (A car park and the* ***Wheatsheaf*** *are 150m R). Carry on ahead (200m).*

ⓕ *At the end of the fields go L to the road, across and through the trees to the military fence (150m). Follow the boundary track back L (600m) and round the corner.* ➜⑥

⑤ After the roundabout (200m) take the path L to the corner of the army fence (70m) and down L of it.

⑥ Stay on the boundary track with the fence (converging on power lines) to the low point with side track (1000m). Go on, past a pylon L, up to the crest of the rise with a path L opposite a gate (100m). ❇

⑦ Take the side path L through the heath (120m). Cross the road and take the path opposite which soon bends L up the slope (150m). At the bend in the farm drive, bear L along the boundary track (150m).

⑧ Go R round the corner of the fence and carry on in a straight line to the top of the ridge (550m).

⑨ Follow the ridge path R past the **sarsen** to the very end of the ridge (220m) then descend the stepped path R (50m) and, at the bottom of the steps, go L on the second crosspath to the end (150m).

⑩ Turn R along the wide path gently down through heath (400m). At the end curve R on the track which bends L and drops to the Leisure Centre car parks (150m).

⑪ Cross the car parks parallel with the boundary fence R and continue on the path through trees diverging from the fence to the Leisure Centre road (150m). Keep on beside the road to the pond at the bottom corner of Lightwater Country Park (200m). ★

⑫ Turn L after the pond and follow the wide path along the R edge of two ponds (250m).

⑬ At the third pond turn L across the end (70m). Just after the foot-bridge turn L (10m) then R. At the next path junction (50m), bear L (10m) then R. Continue on this path to the parking area under the trees (100m), up into the sports field and along the R edge (100m).

⑭ Halfway along the field, exit R over the cartbridge and follow the wide path ahead over the heath to the motorway footbridge (250m).

⑮ Cross the motorway (100m) and take the small path L beside it skirting behind the houses of **Bagshot** past the end of a road (150m). Continue behind gardens, with a zigzag (100m). After the houses the path converges on the motorway then diverges towards the water tower (400m).

⑯ At the track system, turn R up the boundary path over the hill and down to the **railway** (Ascot-Ash Vale) (500m). Stay ahead to the bridge (near the A30) (300m). ❇

⑰ Turn L up the path to the car park and Maultway (300m).

14 Windlesham, village and arboretum

About 6½ km/4 miles; through Windlesham arboretum, the village and fields; gentle inclines. The shorter version of 3½ km/2½ miles avoids the village. OS Maps 1:25000 160 Windsor, 1:50000 175 Reading.

Start from Windlesham Church, SU 930 637. The layby at the church holds about 20 cars but fills up during church functions. Trust members may use the arboretum car park, SU 932 627.

The Surrey Cricketers ☎ 01276 472192
The Half Moon ☎ 01276 473329

Linking walk 10★

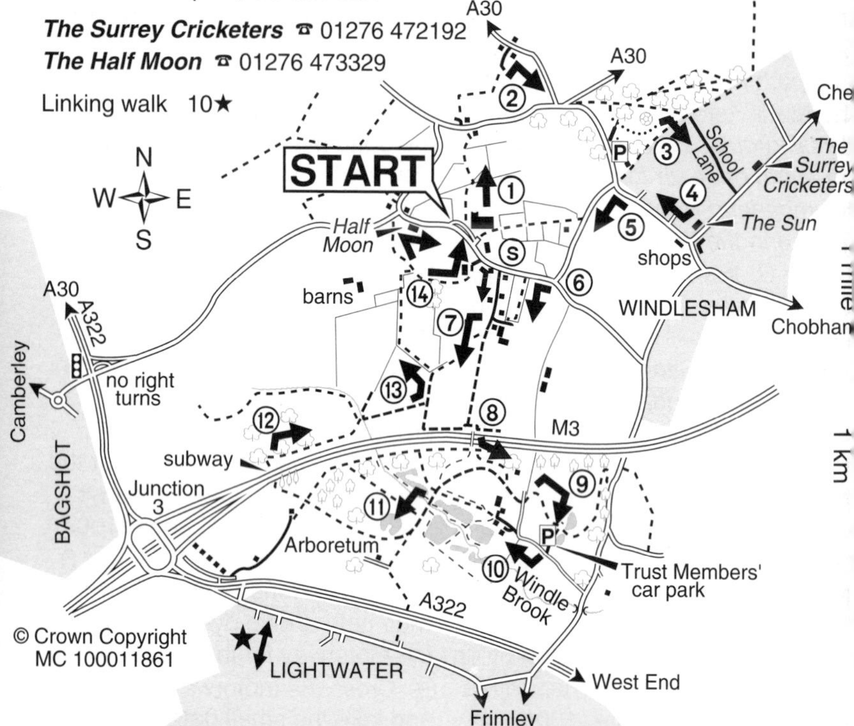

Ⓢ *Shorter version: Go past the church (100m) and R on Rectory Lane (200m).* ➔⑦

① Take the diagonal path across the middle of the main part of the churchyard then L to the next road (350m). Cross to the house drive, slightly L and carry on on the winding path between fields to the next road (400m).

② Walk along the road R (400m). At the end turn L across the end of the next side road (40m) and take the oblique path L under the trees (100m). At the first opportunity turn R out of the trees to the open sports field and cross the grass to the furthest corner L beyond the children's play area (300m).

③ At the end of the field, turn R along the track between the houses (School Lane) to the road (300m). (The ***Surrey Cricketers*** is L 100m.) Go R down Chertsey Road to the shops (250m).

④ Turn R and walk up Updown Hill through the middle of **Windlesham** (350m).

⑤ Take Pound Lane, L, to the main road (350m).

⑥ Go R up the main road (100m). Before the houses enter the narrow field L. Follow the L edge to the end (150m) and go R on the track to the lane (50m). Turn L (50m).

⑦ At the end carry on straight ahead (not R) down the track at the L edge of the field (300m).

⑧ Cross the motorway footbridge. (100m) but don't continue ahead. Turn L but then fork R away from the motorway on the path into the **arboretum** (200m). Join the track to the tarmac drive L (50m).

⑨ Cross the drive and turn L on the track diverging from it. Carry on round the trees to the pond (250m) or explore more widely.

⑩ Turn R through the members' car park to the arboretum main drive (100m) and R along the drive to the house gates (100m). Take the path ahead through the middle of the arboretum (200m).

⑪ At the crossing path, turn L to pass between ponds and over the **Windle** Brook (200m). Swing R past the C-shaped pond towards South Farm visible in the distance (400m) ★ and continue on the path under the motorway (200m).

⑫ Follow the footpath beside the motorway R (300m) then bear L and continue ahead along the cart track to the T-junction (200m).

⑬ Turn L along the fenced track (100m). At the R bend, enter the field L. Follow the L edge to the bend and on along the second side then continue up the fenced path bending R to a T-junction (400m).

⑭ Either go R to the road then L or go L to the road then R past the ***Half Moon*** to Windlesham Church (500m).

Railways in this book:

The **London-Southampton** main line was one of the earliest railways for long distance public traffic, preceded only by the Manchester to Liverpool railway (1830) and the South Carolina Railroad (1831). The company initially called itself London to Southampton Railway but soon changed to London & SW. The first service train ran to Woking in 1838, a week before the first on the Great Western Railway (GWR) to Maidenhead and a month before the Manchester-Birmingham railway was completed. The railway reached Basingstoke in 1839. It was also built from Southampton and the two sections met in Winchester in 1840. The London terminus moved from Nine Elms to Waterloo in 1848. The line was quadrupled in 1903.

LSWR a tribute the the London & SW Railway
B Cooper & R Antell 1988 Ian Allan 128pp

The **Reading-Guildford** line was built in 1849 by the Reading, Guildford and Reigate Railway Co (RRGR) and was operated by SE Railways. It used the LSWR tunnel at Guildford to connect with the section along the N Downs.

The **Woking-Farnham** line, a branch of the LSWR main line, was opened in 1870. It met the Guildford-Alton line of 1852 and was a more direct London link than the Guildford-Farnham line via Tongham which closed in 1937.

The **Staines-Wokingham** railway was built in 1856 by the LSWR as a branch of the Windsor line from Waterloo. At Wokingham it joined the SE Railway's Reading-Guildford line and so linked Reading to Waterloo.

The **Ascot-Ash Vale** line was opened by the LSWR in 1878 connecting Camberley and Bagshot to London and Farnham. It was doubled in 1893.

The **Bisley** Railway was a private 1¼ mile spur from the LSWR at Pirbright built for the National Rifle Association in 1890 and extended 3 miles during World War I for the army camps. It closed in 1952 and its bridge (near Lock 15) was dismantled in 1980.

15 Frimley Green and Deepcut

About 9 km/5½ miles or 1 km/½ mile less; along the Basingstoke Canal and across heathland. The heathland part is an army training ground where public are free to wander but shooting (blanks) and thunder flashes) may disturb dogs and owners. OS maps 1:25000 145 Guildford, 1:50000 186 Aldershot.

Start from Frimley Lodge Park car park, SU 888 562.

Linking walks 16✳ 17✪ 35❇

Kings Head ☎ 01252 835431 **Basingstoke Canal Centre** ☎ 01252 370073

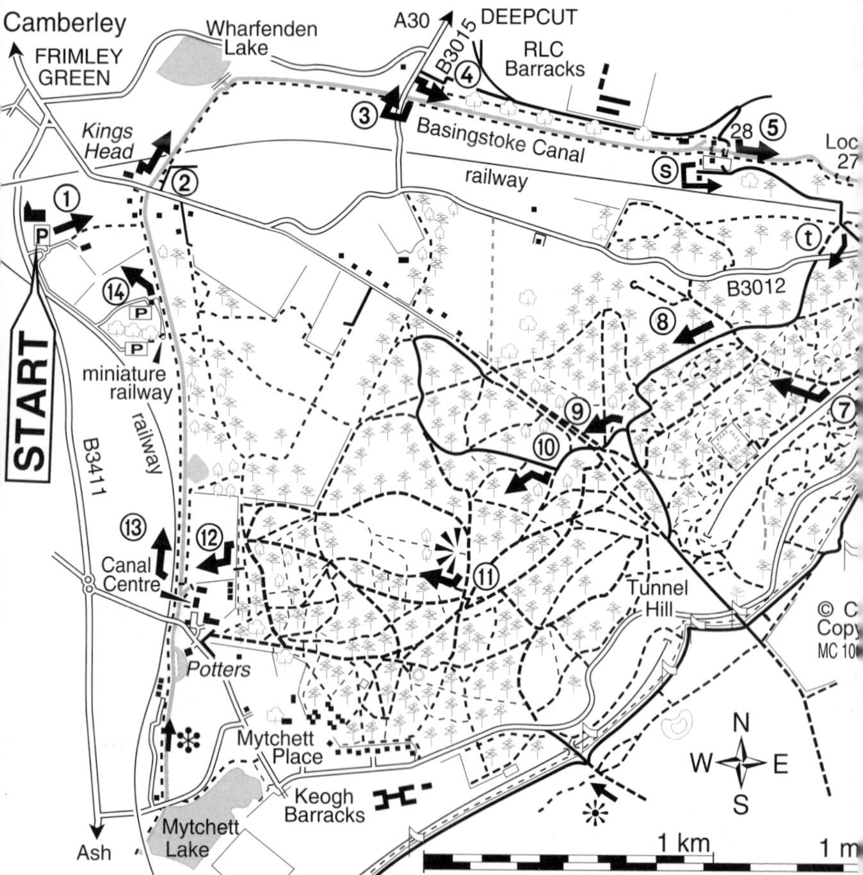

① From Frimley Lodge car park join the track to the pavilion and continue L of it along the boundary to the **Basingstoke Canal** (300m). Turn L along the tow path to the road bridge (100m).

② Take the path L up to the road and cross the canal (100m). Turn into the drive L (30m). Skirt round the garden of **Frimhurst** Lodge and keep on beside the canal over the aqueduct (100m) and on to **Wharfenden** Lake (300m). Carry on round the bends (as the canal turns out of the Blackwater valley) to the next road bridge (600m).

③ Go under the bridge, up the steps R (100m) and over the canal to the track R opposite Highbridge House (150m).

④ Follow the track into the wood. At the 1st bend (100m) turn off R on the path to the edge of the canal cutting (50m) then follow it along the edge of the deep cut to the canal workshop (850m). Go through the workshop yard and take the track down R to Lock 28 (150m). Cross the footbridge.

Ⓢ Slightly shorter version: Turn R along the towpath to the end of the wall (80m) then L up the path away from the canal (80m). At the house turn L along the drive and follow it through the wood and round the R bend over the 4-track railway (600m).

ⓣ After the bridge fork R up the lesser track (100m). Continue over the road, up, round R over a hill, down to a 4-way track (500m) and ahead. ➜⑧

⑤ Follow the towpath L to Lock 25 at **Curzon Bridges** (900m). ✪

⑥ Ascend and cross the **railway** bridge (London-Southampton). Go on to the road, where there is a **pillbox** (200m). Don't pass under the **railway** (Woking-Farnham line) but walk along the road R (100m) then diverge on the track L. Disregard the side track under the bridge L (150m) ❄❄ and continue up beside the railway (400m).

⑦ Stay on the same track when it curves away from the railway up a valley. Keep on to the major cross track just after the ridge (500m). Turn L.

⑧ Follow the track over a ridge disregarding several side tracks but round L & R bends (500m).

⑨ At the next L bend fork R to 2 major crossing tracks, the second being Old Guildford Road (100m). Cross the OGR ahead to the track which curves L. Don't turn off from the curve (70m) but keep on to the next junction (100m).

⑩ Turn R with the main track (100m) then take the 1st track L which descends to meet a larger track (300m). Turn L up onto the ridge (100m). Disregard the wide branching track back down R. See the view and carry on. Turn onto the next major track R (200m) (or cut the corner on small paths down through the heath).

⑪ Follow this undulating track to a complex junction of tracks and paths (450m) and turn R on the major track, down off the hill. At the bottom (250m) cross the wide track and go straight through the trees to the fence (50m).

⑫ Turn L along the fence to the gate (80m) then cross the field slightly L to the Canal Centre (200m). Cross the canal to the towpath and turn R. The swing bridge is open to walkers only 11am-4pm. If it is not open go out L to the road (100m), R over the canal (100m) and back on the other side.

⑬ Follow the towpath to Frimley Lodge Park. The **railway** L is the Ascot-Farnham line. Keep on as far as the end of the **miniature railway** track (1000m) then

⑭ leave the canal and cross the sports fields diagonally back to the car park (350m).

16 Tunnel Hill and the blasted heath

This walk is often not possible. Most days red flags are flown at entrances to the ranges. Flags stay down some week ends and during holidays at Christmas, Easter and August. The range office is on 01252-325233.

About 7 km/ 4¼ miles; mostly through open heath with hilly paths; best in August or bleak mid-winter. Extensions of 1½ km/1 mile & 1 km/¾ mile; a short cut of 1½ km/1 mile. OS maps 1:25000 145 Guildford, 1:50000 186 Aldershot.

Start from the larger roadside parking area between the road junctions, SU 918 557. Most of the gateways to the ranges have parking spots.

Linking walks 15✳ 17✪ 35✧ 36✺ 37✦

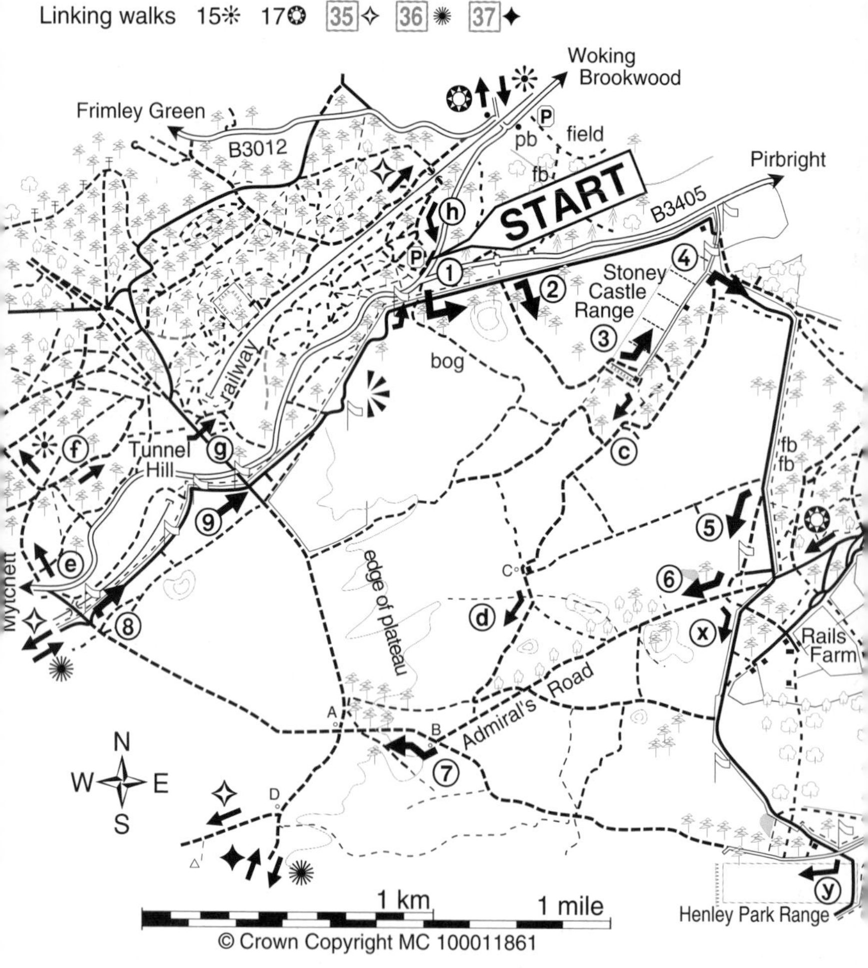

✪① From the parking area cross both roads. Go up the track from the junction, in through the fence of the army land (100m). Follow the boundary track down L (300m).

② Take the 1st side track R round a L bend (400m) to the butts of Stoney Castle rifle range (200m). Follow the track across the front of the butts (100m).

ⓒ *Short cut of 1½ km/1mile: From the end of the sand bank behind the targets take the small side path down through the trees (50m). At the wider path turn R (100m). Stay ahead at the track disregarding several side tracks (500m).*

ⓓ *Go round an abrupt L bend then a ½R bend with side track (100m) and descend to the hairpin bend (400m). Use the path ahead to join to the next major track (50m) and go on, R, to an oblique T-junction (150m) then R.* ➧⑦

③ Walk down the hard track beside the range (400m).

④ Near the bottom turn R on the tarmac side road which soon becomes a track (350m). Carry on round the R bend then along the boundary track until it bends slightly L (600m).

⑤ Diverge R up the track onto the hillock (300m) and drop straight down the other side (50m).

ⓧ *Extension of 1½ km/1 mile: Re-join the boundary track outside the fence (100m) and carry on to the next rifle range (Henley Park Range) (1000m).* ✦

ⓨ *Turn back R up the tarmac drive beside the range (400m). After the butts keep on up the track over a rise (350m), up round an S-bend and to the side track back R (700m). Keep on ahead.* ➧⑦

⑥ Turn R on the major track from the boundary fence (Admiral's Road). Pass through the trees then over a rise. Disregard side paths and keep on up to the oblique T-junction (1100m). Turn R.

⑦ Follow the track up onto the **plateau**, over the 1st cross track (which leads L to a good picnic spot with views) and the 2nd cross track (350m). ✧✷ Keep on ahead over the plateau then gently down to the boundary near the **railway** (Woking-Farnham) (1000m). ✧

ⓔ *Extension of 1 km/¾ mile: Carry on over the boundary and the railway bridge down to the road (150m). Cross and go up the track opposite which curves R to a complex junction (300m).* ✳

ⓕ *Take the uphill track ahead skirting the hill R (300m). At the top, fork R then stay ahead until the level long straight track (Old Guildford Road) (250m).*

ⓖ *Cross and continue on the path ahead soon passing the tunnel mouth (out of sight L). Stay near the railway cutting and drop off the edge of the hill (350m). Skirt round the base of the next hill near the railway (300m). When the track bends R into a little cleft, go up the track parallel with the railway, on the little ridge then down L as if to pass under the railway (500m).*

ⓗ *Don't go under the bridge but return (50m) and bear L on the main track up the valley. Watch out for the side path L (150m) and ascend the valley side through the pines to the parking spot (100m).*

⑧ Follow the boundary track up R past the tunnel mouth (550m) and R round a bend to the next cross track, near the road (200m).

⑨ Keep on along the boundary. Either keep to the track when it loops away from the boundary to avoid the steepest inclines or go over the top (700m). After the 2nd peak descend to the next cross track (100m) and exit L to the road junction and parking spot (100m).

17 Pirbright and the Basingstoke Canal

About 9 km/5½ miles, mainly level, along the canal and over fields; shady. If the red flags are down the route can be extended 1 km/¾ km through the army ranges. OS maps 1:25000 145 Guildford, 1:50000 186 Aldershot.

Start at Pirbright from the car park on the village green, SU 946 560, or at the larger roadside parking area between the road junctions, SU 918 557.

Linking walks 15✪ 16✪ 35★ 40❀ 1✦ 3✿

The White Hart ☎ 01483 799029 ***The Cricketers*** ☎ 01483 473198

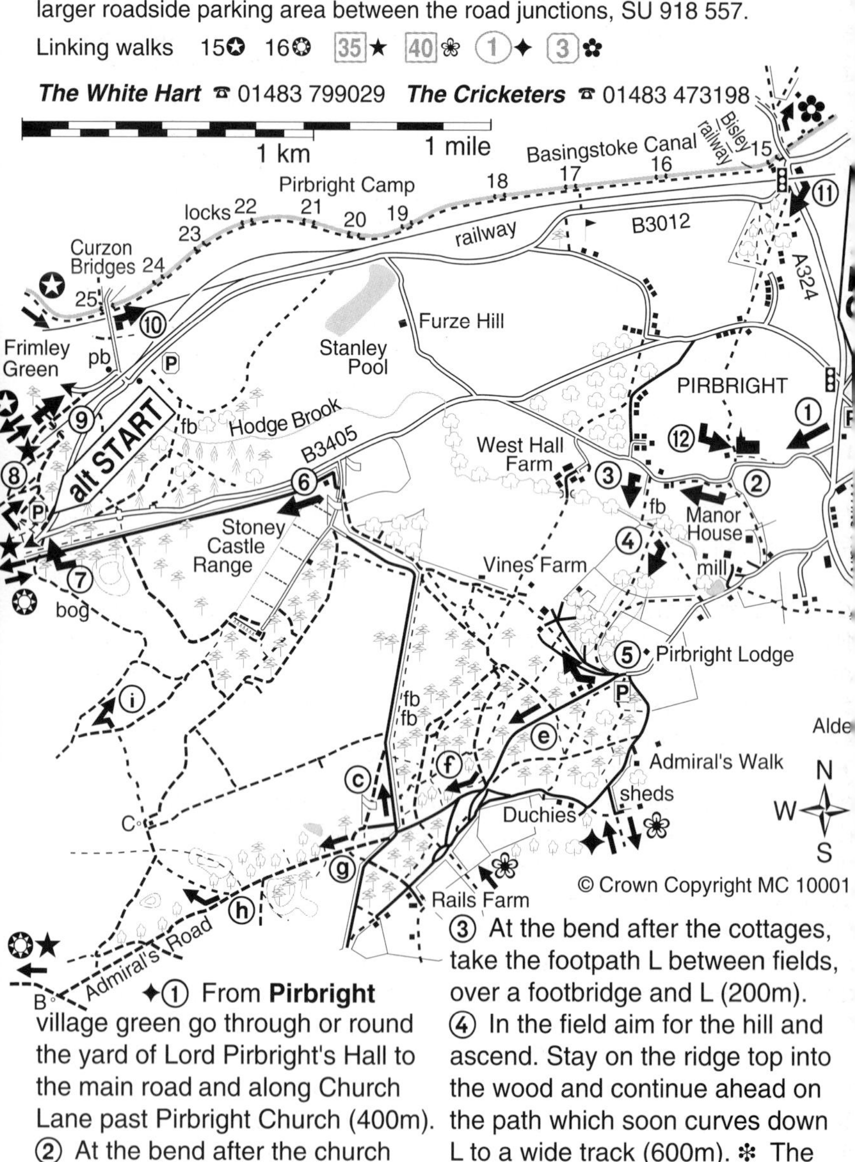

✦① From **Pirbright** village green go through or round the yard of Lord Pirbright's Hall to the main road and along Church Lane past Pirbright Church (400m).

② At the bend after the church (100m) enter the field L but carry on beside the lane (200m) to the house then on the lane (100m).

③ At the bend after the cottages, take the footpath L between fields, over a footbridge and L (200m).

④ In the field aim for the hill and ascend. Stay on the ridge top into the wood and continue ahead on the path which soon curves down L to a wide track (600m). ❊ The main route is R from here but to see **Pirbright Lodge**, go L along the lane (100m) then return.

ⓔ *Extension of 1km/¾ mile into the military ranges if the red flags are down: Take the wide level track continuing straight ahead from the end of the tarmac past houses R (200m) and eventually down to a 6-way junction (600m).*

ⓕ *Bear R on the rising track to the fence of the ranges (400m).*

ⓒ *If the red flags are flying don't go on but follow the fence R all the way to the road (1400m). ➔⑧*

ⓖ *The track bends to follow the boundary. Take the onward track through the fence into the dip and up the next slope. On top pass the track L after the hillock (450m). ✪★*

ⓗ *Soon after this (100m) take the diverging path R to the next major vehicle track (300m). Follow this R to the bend at the sunken hut (150m) then take the branch path ahead to the next track (300m).*

ⓘ *Go L up to the track junction (200m) then down R (300m). When the track branches, fork L and go on round the L bends down to a boggy area and up to the boundary (500m). ➔⑦*

⑤ Go along the curving track over a little rise towards Vines Farm (200m). Just round the R curve, diverge on the path L soon passing between a house and the farm (100m). Keep on outside the fields. A lesser path under the trees avoids winter the mud of the track. Eventually the track runs beside the fence of Stoney Castle Ranges to the road (900m).

⑥ Turn L and follow the fence of the ranges to the next exit track. If red flags are flying stay outside the fence; if not, use the boundary track (1100m). ★

⑦ Go out to the road junction and into the trees opposite (50m).

⑧ Drop straight down into the hollow to a junction of numerous tracks and paths (100m) then either follow the track down the valley R or climb to the next ridge and follow that down R to pass under the **railway** (Pirbright-Farnham line) (350m). ✪

⑨ Turn R down the track (150m) and keep on ahead at the road (100m). Don't pass under the next railway bridge but turn L near the **pillbox** along the tarmac track to **Curzon Bridges**. Cross the bridge over the main line (London-Southampton) **railway** (200m).

⑩ Drop to the towpath R. Follow the **Basingstoke Canal** passing below Pirbright Camp L.

Pirbright Camp was the depot of the Guards regiments (Scots, Welsh, Irish, Grenadier, Coldstream), infantry units whose duties include guarding the Royal Household. The 3000 acres of wasteland was bought by the Brigade of Guards in the 1870s. Since reorganisation it has become barracks for training recruits to all regiments.

Just before Lock 15 at the road see the pillars and banks of the former Bisley **Railway** (2500m). ✿

⑪ Join the road at the next canal bridge and go R under the railway. At the road junction, take the footpath R in the angle of the roads through the wood, across a road and on past fields to Pirbright Church (1100m).

⑫ Before the road turn L to the church. Go right along the churchyard past **Stanley**'s grave (large lump of granite) then along the road to the village green (500m). ✦

18 Mattingley to Rotherwick

About 8½ km/5½ miles with a version 1 km/¾ mile shorter, through fields and wood; gentle inclines; lots of stiles, muddy in winter; half shady. OS maps 1:25000 144 Basingstoke, 1:50000 186 Aldershot or 175 Reading.

Start at Mattingley Church, SU 736 580. For the shorter version it is best to start from Rotherwick, parking at the roadside near the church, SU 712 562.

Linking walks 19❇ 21☆ ㉖★ ㉗✷ ㉘❖ ㉙✺

The Coach & Horses ☎ 0870 240 1135 ***The Falcon*** ☎ 01256 762586
Leather Bottle ☎ 0188 932 6371

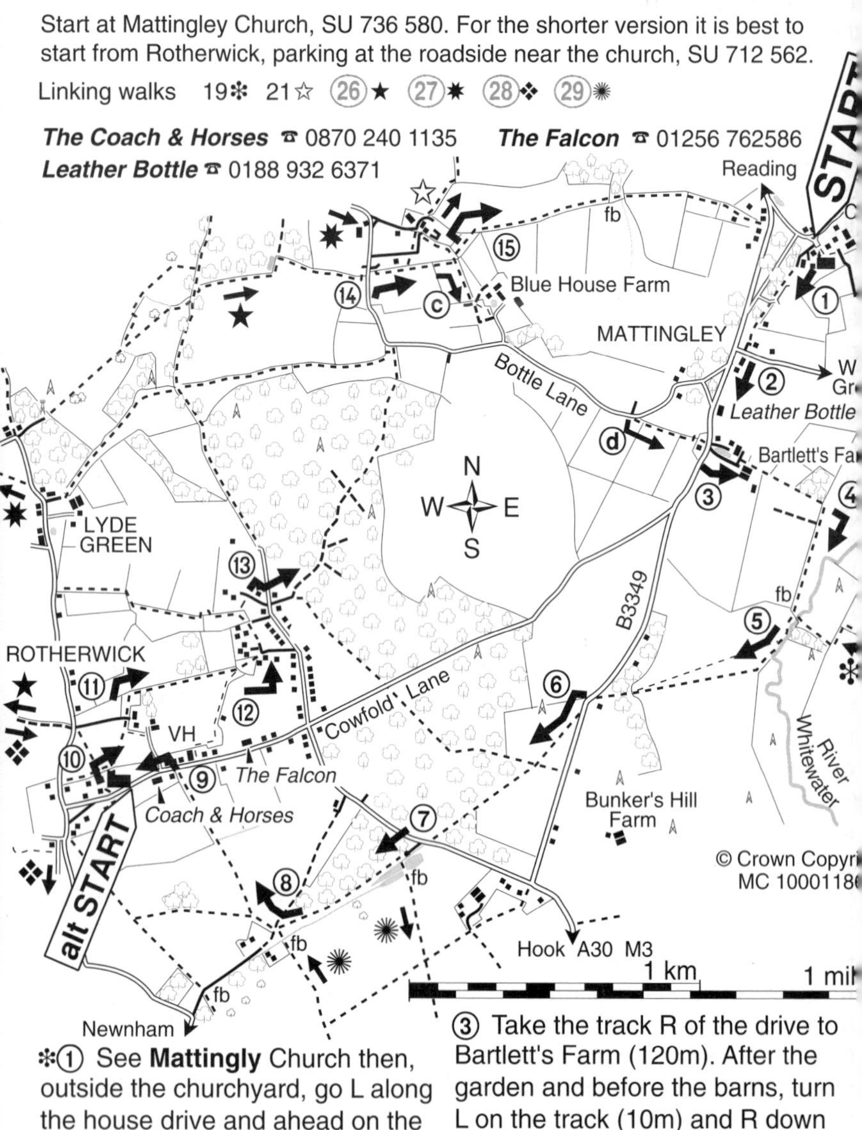

❇① See **Mattingly** Church then, outside the churchyard, go L along the house drive and ahead on the path under trees, across another house drive, to the road (450m).

② Over the grass go on along the main road past the ***Leather Bottle*** (200m) to Bartlett's Farm L (120m).

③ Take the track R of the drive to Bartlett's Farm (120m). After the garden and before the barns, turn L on the track (10m) and R down the path between fields (300m).

④ In the bottom field turn R along the hedge to the end (350m). Just round the corner disregard the footbridge and go through the rees beside the Whitewater **River** nto the next field (100m).

⑤ The right of way follows the iver to the L bend (100m) then the ence ahead to the L bend (70m) hen turns R up the field (but the oath is often more direct). Aim for he 2nd pylon R of the hilltop farm o an indent in the top edge (400m) and go on through the belt of trees oetween fields to the road (150m).

⑥ Cross the road. Go L round the bend along the verge (100m) then take the path diverging R over the field to the corner of the wood, midway along the edge of the field (200m). In the next field carry on along the edge of the trees to the corner (250m) and ahead through the wood to the road (300m).

⑦ Slightly R (15m) take the track opposite. After the anglers' car park keep on beside the trees to the track near houses (550m). ✷

⑧ Cross the track into the field. Follow the garden hedge L to the end (100m) then bear R over the field to the hedge-end (250m) and carry on ahead to the road (250m).

⑨ Turn L to the ***Coach & Horses*** (50m) and church (200m). ★❖✷

⑩ Go through **Rotherwick** church yard to the field behind (80m). Turn R along the bottom hedge to the end of the churchyard (50m) then up L over the field to the corner of the garden (120m). Continue outside the garden, across the farm track and through the next small field to the hedge (100m).

⑪ Turn R at the hedge and follow it down to the bottom of the next large field. Go out through the small field to the road between houses (450m).

⑫ Turn L to the parking area of Wedmans Place and carry on along the footpath over a drive to the field (100m). Cross the end of the field diagonally (50m).

⑬ Exit along the narrow path beside the garden (50m) then R on the drive (80m). Cross the lane and go on along the track into the wood (100m). Stay ahead on track and path to the far edge (850m). Cross the field to the lane (100m). On the lane, turn L. Go round the bend and up to the first house drive R (250m). ☆

⑭ Just into the drive enter the field R. Follow the L edge of the paddocks to the end hedge (300m).

ⓒ *Shorter version: Go R round the corner and along the L edge to Blue House Farm (150m). Skirt round outside the garden to the tarmac drive and exit R (200m). Go L up Bottle Lane (500m).*

ⓓ *When the lane curves L enter the field R but continue in the same direction beside the L hedge (250m). Near the house, cross into the side field L and go out to the main road in Mattingley (50m). (The **Leather Bottle** is L 100m.) Cross and continue ahead.* ➧③

⑮ Cross into the field L. Along the hedge (20m) turn R into the small side field and exit at the opposite end (80m). Follow the edge R to the end (500m) and cross the little wooded valley (50m). Carry on at the L edge of more fields then between houses (600m). Cross the road and follow the path through the trees. Stay ahead on the lane round L to the church (250m).

19 Mattingley and West Green

About 7½ km/4½ with a short cut of 2 km/1¼ miles miles; farmland, mainly pasture; muddy in winter, not much shade in summer; lots of stiles.
OS maps 1:25000 144 Basingstoke, 1:50000 186 Aldershot or 175 Reading.

Start from Mattingley Church, SU 736 580, or from the road-junction near the *Leather Bottle* (park on the green), SU 733 577, or at West Green (park under the trees beside the lane opposite the house), SU 746 563.

Linking walks 18✻ 20✦ 21✳ 22✡ 23❀

The Leather Bottle ☎ 0188 932 6371

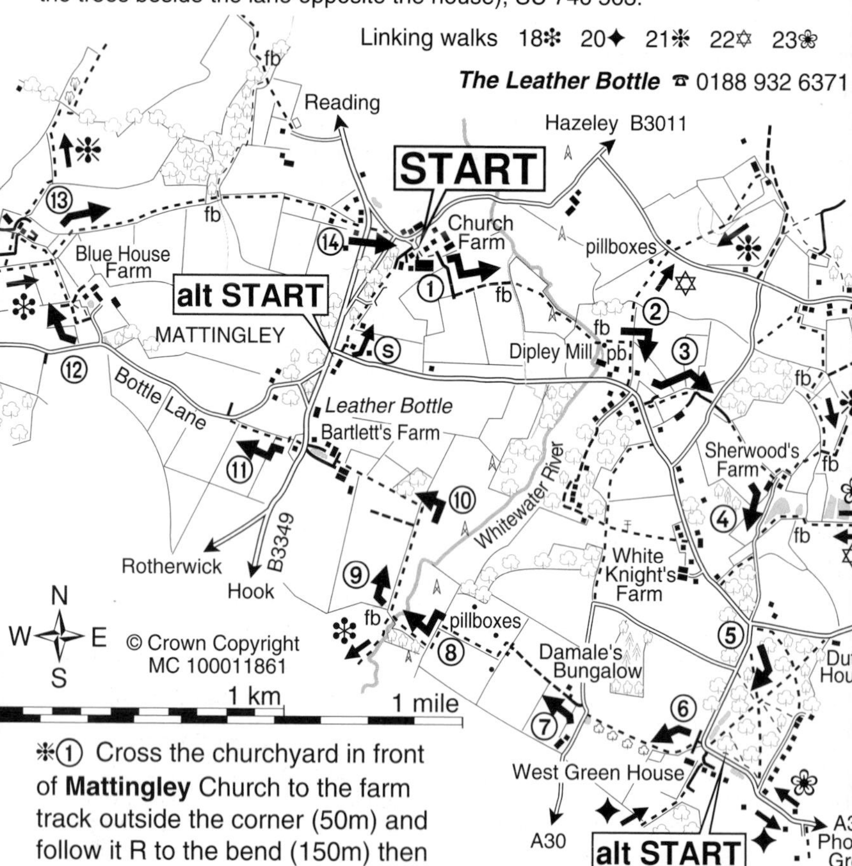

✻① Cross the churchyard in front of **Mattingley** Church to the farm track outside the corner (50m) and follow it R to the bend (150m) then L to the field (200m). Cross ½R to the bank of the Whitewater **River**. Stay beside it through the next field to the footbridge L near the buildings of **Dipley Mill** (350m).

② Cross the river. Go round the **pillbox** and straight over the field to the hedge (100m) ✡ then R to the road (150m). (The mill is best seen from the hump-backed bridge 100m along the road R.)

③ Up the road L, round the bend, (80m) turn L into the track and stay ahead along the L edges of the fields (150m). Join the track out to the lane (80m). Cross and go on along the track then over the field beside the L hedge. Exit from the field near the houses at Sherwood Farm (300m). ❀

④ Go R along the tarmac drive to the road junction (500m).

⑤ Follow the road opposite to the bend (50m) then bear L between the trees to the cross path on the causeway (200m) ✦ and R back to the road at the pond (250m).

⑥ Cross the road at the bend to the field R. Follow the L hedge past **West Green** House then the line of trees to the road (400m).

⑦ On the other side, slightly R, continue on the cart track past Damale's Bungalow (350m). At the end enter the field ahead (with pillboxes) and skirt around the L edge to the bottom (300m).

⑧ Turn L along the bottom of the next field (80m). Before the next corner cross the ditch R. Go along the L edge, over the river and up to the hedge (200m). ❇

⑨ Follow the hedge R. Disregard the farm track L (300m) but turn L on the footpath soon after it (60m).

⑩ At the farm buildings (300m) don't continue into the farmhouse garden but join the farm track L (10m) and go out to the road, R (100m). (The ***Leather Bottle*** is 100m along the road R.)

Ⓢ *Cut of 2km/1¼ mile: Walk past the pub to the side road R (200m). Just into the side road (30m) turn off on the 1st drive L and continue on the path to the church (450m).*

⑪ Cross the little field opposite and continue through successive fields on the L side of the hedge (250m) then along the lane (500m).

⑫ Start along the tarmac drive of Blue House Farm R (100m) but turn off L at the garden wall and skirt L of the homestead (100m). In the first field after it, follow the R fence to the corner (120m). ❇

⑬ Don't turn L on the right of way along the hedge. Go on briefly in the field ahead (20m) then turn R into the small side field and exit at the opposite end (80m). Turn R and follow the hedge to the end of the field (500m). Cross the small wooded valley (50m) and carry on ahead, now at the L edge, through more fields, then between houses to the road (600m).

⑭ Cross the road and follow the footpath through the trees to the lane near the church (250m).

West Green was presented to the National Trust by Sir Victor Sassoon in 1957. The house is leased but the gardens are open to the public, Wednesday to Sunday in summer. The house was bombed in 1990, supposedly by the IRA, but the resident, Alisdair McAlpine, an ex-Chairman of the Conservative Party, had left a week earlier. It was probably a 17th century farm house but was rebuilt for "Hangman" Hawley in the 1740s.

General Henry Hawley 1679-1759 may have been an illegitimate son of George I. He became a professional soldier and saw action in Ireland and Flanders as a cavalry officer. His renown came from the Scottish rebellion of 1745 for Bonny Prince Charlie. His own troopers called him "Hangman" for leaving rebels on gibbets in Edinburgh weeks after execution. He lost the Battle of Falkirk because he was decoyed to a dinner party at the time of the rebels' attack. At Culloden, the final battle, he was cavalry commander under the Duke of Cumberland and exhorted his men to kill the wounded. He hung deserters and followed the rebel clans to destroy their homes so they would not rebel again. *Culloden* John Prebble Secker & Warburg 1961 367pp

20 West Green and Hook Mill

About 6½ km/4 miles with an extension of 1 km/¾ mile; undulating farmland. Some of the paths disappear at ploughing time. Boggy near the river in winter. Not much shade. OS maps 1:25000 144 Basingstoke, 1:50000 186 Aldershot.

Linking walks 19✦ 22❃ 23✪ 34✿ (29)☆

Start near West Green House, SU 746 563, (park under the trees beside the lane outside) or at the *Crooked Billet* on the A30, SU 737 548.

The Crooked Billet ☎ 01256 762118

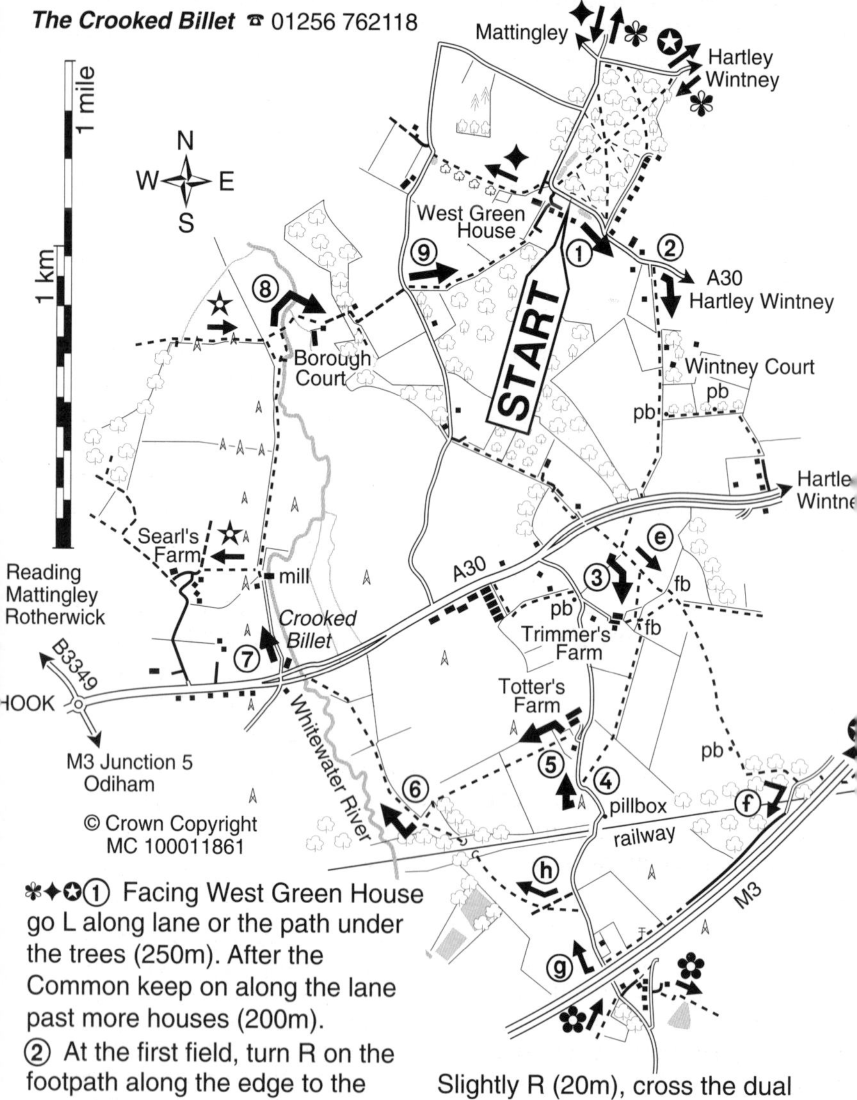

❃✦✪① Facing West Green House go L along lane or the path under the trees (250m). After the Common keep on along the lane past more houses (200m).

② At the first field, turn R on the footpath along the edge to the trees (250m). Carry on at the L edge of the fields and out past the gas enclosure to the road (550m). Slightly R (20m), cross the dual carriageway and go through the field diagonally R to the path under the trees (150m).

ⓔ *Extension of 1 km/¾ mile: Turn L. Stay on the path between the fields past a* **pillbox** *R near the top of the fields (800m) then round L through trees to the end near the motorway cutting (300m).*

ⓕ *Turn R along the disused road (100m). Cross the* **railway** *bridge* (London-Southampton) *and stay beside the motorway fence all the way down to the road (800m).* ✿

ⓖ *Walk up the lane R (200m).*

ⓗ *Just before the end of the field L take the path across the corner (100m), over the track and up in the same line to the trees in the corner of the next field (300m). Pass under the railway (50m) and keep on to the hedge corner R (150m).* ➜⑥

③ Turn L but look out for a bridge R (100m) to the fields. Aim for the hedge corner 100m L of the barns but cross the footbridge L before it (150m). Cross the R corner of the next field (50m) and walk up the fields, R of the fence, over the hilltop. In the last field aim 50m R of the pylon (550m).

④ Walk along the lane R to Totter's Farm (200m).

⑤ Turn L through the gateway and stay ahead over fences and under power cables (300m). Carry on along the middle of the large field. If the path is obscure aim for the R end of the trees just over the brow (150m) and drop to the hedge corner (70m). Go down the L side of the hedge to the bottom (80m) and round the external corner R.

⑥ Follow the hedge, along the edge of the Whitewater valley (300m). In the next field diverge L from the hedge making for the apparent middle of the end fence (150m), then more L, towards the pub and the road bridge (200m).

⑦ Cross the dual carriageway to the ***Crooked Billet*** (100m). ☆ Walk along the tarmac drive L of the pub (350m). After Mill Cottage L take the narrow path beside the drive. Don't turn L up into the side field (unless you want to look over the hedge which hides **Hook Mill** in summer) but keep on to the field beyond (100m). Go straight on along the L hedge until it meets the river (500m) then follow the river bank (200m). Don't cross the cart bridge R or diverge on the path along the hedge L. Stay on the river bank round the bends and on to the next footbridge (200m).

⑧ Cross the river and bear L over the field (50m) to cross another bridge then turn R and make your way up through the paddocks to the track from **Borough Court** house (150m) and up the slope. Follow the track round R & L bends and up to the road (300m).

⑨ Cross the road and carry on along the path which skirts R of the field then the garden of West Green to the car park (600m). Walk out to your parking place.

Hook Mill on the Whitewater River is probably on the site of one of the nine mills recorded in the Domesday Book for the manor of Odiham. Documents indicate there was a mill here in 1561 but the present building is 17th century. At that time it was a paper mill, the water power being used to pulp cotton and linen rags in alkali. By 1830 the use of water mills for paper making had largely ceased and it was a flour mill until the 1900s. It was converted to a house about 1920.

Hook's Watermill Glynis Wilsdon 1986 12pp

21 Mattingley, Hound Green and Hazeley Heath

About 8½ km/5½ miles with a short cut of 1km/¾ mile; undulating fields and heath; lots of stiles; half shady; usually good in winter. Hazeley Heath paths are confusing. OS maps 1:25000 144 Basingstoke, 1:50000 186 or 175.

Start at Mattingley Church, SU 736 580, or at the roadside opposite the *Shoulder of Mutton*, SU 742 590, just off the B3011.

Linking walks 19✻ 21☆ 22✿ 25★

Shoulder of Mutton 0118 932 6272
The Leather Bottle 0118 932 6371

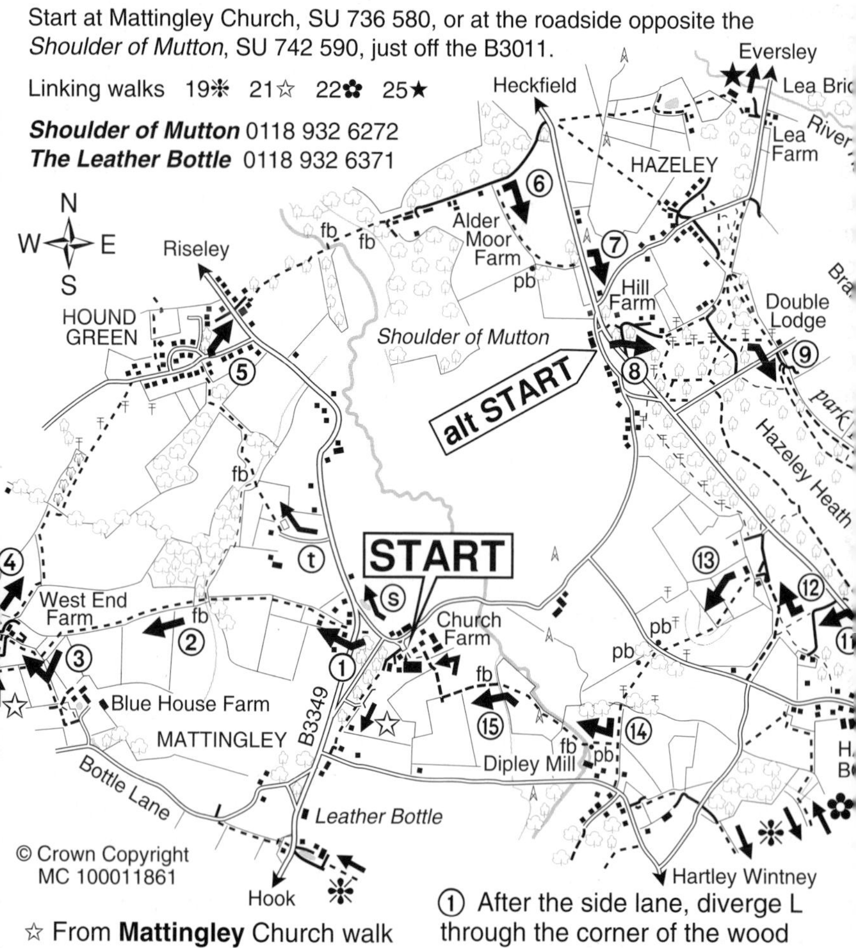

☆ From **Mattingley** Church walk out to the lane and L (100m).

Ⓢ *Shorter version: Keep on round to the main road (100m) then R along it (250m).*

Ⓣ *Turn L up the Lynchmere Farm drive (200m). Almost at the house take the path R, twixt garden and tennis court, down to the brook in the trees (200m) and up between fields and gardens to Hound Green (450m). Turn R.* ➜⑤

① After the side lane, diverge L through the corner of the wood (50m). Stay ahead over the main road and between the houses then along the R edge of the fields to the little wooded valley (500m).

② Keep on ahead and along the L edge of the next field (550m).

③ At the curve before West End farm look out for a stile L and cross the little field to the next one (80m). Turn R along the edge, skirting the buildings and garden (150m).

④ Cross the drive and turn R. Don't head for the road but go on past the buildings to the first field (70m). Follow the R edge to the corner (150m). In the next field skirt round the L edge and exit at the end corner of the wood (250m). Follow the edge of the wood along the next field (200m). When it ends keep on in the same direction to the electricity pole seen between the nearest houses (300m). Walk on along the lane (250m).

⑤ At the green cross the grass obliquely to the far L corner (200m). Go over the main road and down the track next to the garage (50m). Before the last house turn R on the path skirting the garden. Continue between the fields (300m). and over the Whitewater **River**. Go on across the valley beside the fence. After the stream ascend through the trees. Stay ahead on the track past farm buildings (550m). ★

⑩★ B3011 HW

⑥ Just after the house (50m) turn R up the edge of the field. Stay beside the fence curving L to the road (550m).

⑦ Cross to the verge opposite and follow the road R (300m).

⑧ Opposite the lane outlet near the ***Shoulder of Mutton***, climb the stepped path up the bank of the main road (50m). At the track go L round the bend and down the R drive (200m). Just after the house turn R to the power lines (30m) then bear L down the heath path with the power lines (200m). Cross the gravel track and keep on, down to the heath boundary at the **park pale** of **Bramshill** (200m).

⑨ Turn R to the double lodge (60m). Cross the drive and carry on beside the boundary, on the track until it bends (50m), then on the path with views of Bramshill House far L (650m). Cross the grass past the pond to the gravel track at the next house (100m). ✿

⑩ Almost immediately (20m) turn R on the path over **Hazeley Heath** (100m). At the cross paths stay ahead between the low hills along the winding path to the horse track near the (audible) road (200m).

⑪ Turn R on the horse track then almost immediately (40m) L on a narrow curving footpath to the road opposite the drive of Hazeley Court (100m). Go along the drive (100m). When it bends L, keep on ahead down the footpath (100m). ✻

⑫ At the 4-way path junction, go R across the slope then up the bridleway to the cottage L (200m).

⑬ Turn L, past the cottage. In the 1st field make for the stile above the bottom L corner and go along the L edge of the 2nd field. In the 3rd field walk out to the brow of the hill then down to the lane, L of the pillbox in the hedge (500m). Slightly R enter the field opposite. Diverge from the R edge to the stile and ditch (200m). In the next field follow the L hedge (100m).

⑭ Before the end, take the side path across the field and over the ditch and river (100m). Follow the bank R into the next field. When the fence bends R, bear L across the field to the gate (300m).

⑮ Go out along the track (200m) and round the R bend (150m). Just before the farm turn L through the churchyard to the car park (100m).

22 Hartford Bridge and Hazeley Bottom

About 8 km/5 miles with a ½ mile extension to Dipley Mill. Mainly over fields but with stretches of heath and oak wood; undulating; lots of stiles; unpleasant in wet seasons. OS maps 1:25000 144 Basingstoke, 1:50000 186 or 175.

Linking walks 19✡ 20❃ 21✿ 23✸ 27❖

Park on the verge in Hares Lane near Hartley Wintney, SU 770 578, or on the verge at Hazeley Bottom, SU 748 579.

White Lion Tea Rooms ☎ 01252 844000

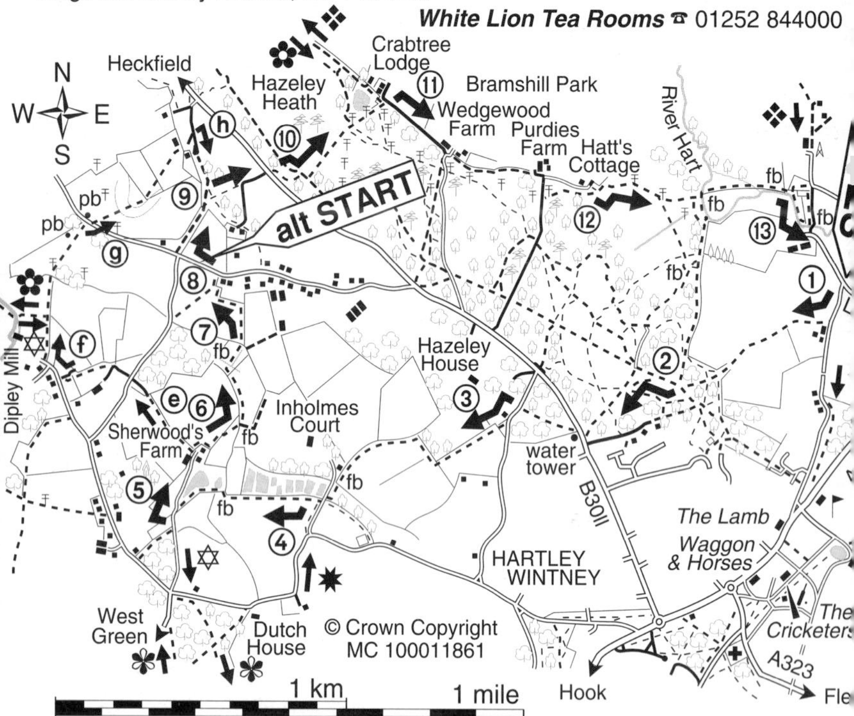

① Follow the side lane (150m). ✸ Just before Hares Farm take the path R between fields and up through the trees to the converging cross path on the flat top (550).

② Go R on the level path as far as the concrete track R (180m) and turn L along the path, opposite, to the road (200m). Cross slightly R (30m) and take the path through the wood to the next road (200m).

③ Turn L along the lane to the house (60m) then bear R along the wall to the field (60m). Go down the R edge (see **Hazeley House** R) (250m). In the 2nd field turn R along the hedge and go on across the end of the 3rd field (120m), round the corner and down the R edge to the bottom (300m). Continue ahead either at the edge of the next field or on the drive from Inholmes Court (80m). ❃

④ Turn R into the 1st field on the other side of the drive. Stay at the R edge to the end (350m) then cross the footbridge and skirt L of the ponds to the drive (150m). ✡

⑤ Walk along the drive R, past Sherwood's Farm (200m).

ⓔ *Extension to* **Dipley Mill** *½ mile: At the end of the farmhouse turn L into the field. Go on along the R edge and out through trees to the lane (300m). Continue on the track opposite (70m). Turn with it into the field L then follow the R hedge to the next road (150m).*

ⓕ *Walk down the road R. Just after the side road L is a footpath R (80m). For a view of Dipley Mill stay on the road to the humped bridge over the Whitewater* **River** *(150m) then return to the footpath. Follow the R edge of the field. Disregard a path L crossing the field (150m) ✿ and go on to the end (150m). Cross the stream and go straight up the next field to the top corner and out to the road (200m).*

ⓖ *Slightly R, enter the field opposite and, ½R, make for the highest point then for the bend in the hedge (150m). Go through to the next field and on in the same direction up the next to exit twixt barn and house (300m).*

ⓗ *On the heath, up from Little Cottage (20m), take the horse track R. Follow it down outside the field to a slight bend (100m) then diverge up the flank of the slope to the cross path (often obscured by fallen leaves) (50m). Turn L up to the bend in the drive from Hazeley Court (100m).* ➔⑩

⑥ In the field after the 2nd house go down the R edge into the next field (30m) then aim L for the gate on the other side at the far end (100m). Over the bridge, follow the hedge and stream L (200m).

⑦ Watch out for a footbridge in mid-field and cross it to the hedge (100m). Disregard the farm track to the barns above. Go up L of the hedge towards the nearest houses (120m) then turn L, and skirt round the gardens to the road in **Hazeley Bottom** (150m).

⑧ Walk along the road L (150m). Opposite the Dipley lane take the path R (200m).

⑨ When it steepens and curves L a little, look for the narrow path R and follow this up through the trees to join the drive from Hazeley Court at a bend (150m).

⑩ Stay ahead to the road and cross to the heath (100m). The path bends R to follow the road briefly then L to a horse track (100m). Go R briefly (30m) then take the path L across **Hazeley Heath** between the slopes. Keep on, disregarding side paths, to the drive at Crabtree Lodge (250m). ❖

⑪ Turn R along the drive under the trees beside the **park pale** of **Bramshill** to Wedgewood Farm (distant views of Bramshill back L) (250m. When it bends R, stay ahead on the bridleway to Purdies Farm (350m) and the drive down to Hatt's Cottage (200m).

⑫ At the end of the tarmac skirt R & L round the corner of the garden in the trees (20m) then turn R across the heath. Disregard side paths up the slope R (300m). Continue into the trees and over the **River** Hart footbridge (50m). Go straight on along the fence over a culvert and footbridge (200m).

⑬ After the footbridge bear R along the river bank to the next footbridge over the river (150m) and cross to the road. Walk along the road L to Hares Lane (200m).

23 Hartley Wintney and West Green

About 10 km/ 6¼ miles; mainly over fields, gently undulating. OS maps 1:25000 144 Basingstoke, 1:50000 186 Aldershot.

Start at the pond at the north end of Hartley Wintney village green, SU 770 569 - roadside parking. Alternatively start at West Green, parking under the trees near the bend, SU 746 563. Winchfield Station is on the route.

Linking walks 19❀ 20✪ 22✱

The Cricketers ☎ 01252 842166 ***The Winchfield Inn*** ☎ 01252 842129

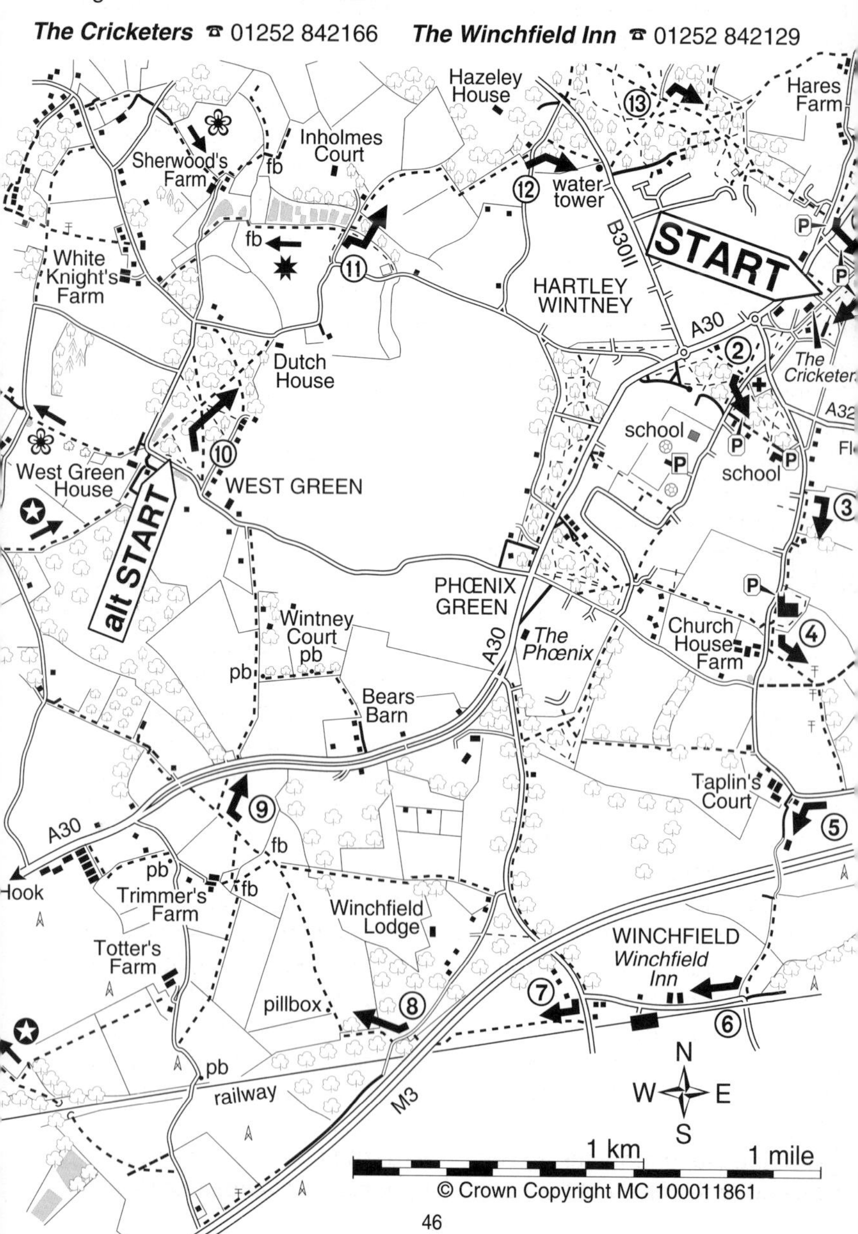

① From the pond, go along the green between the pavilion and the ***Cricketers*** (300m). Carry on in the same direction over the green and the roads to the church (300m).

② Skirt the churchyard then go ½L up through the trees to the top corner of the green (250m) and on along the road at the edge of **Hartley Wintney** (150m).

③ Enter the first field L and follow the path along the edge above the road to the old churchyard (300m). Skirt round the L edge to see the grave of Viscount Alanbrooke and the view (200m) then continue on the path above the road down to Church House Farm (80m).

④ Go L diagonally down to the bottom of the L field; aim for the hedge end in the next field (200m). Cross the track and continue opposite up the L edge of the field to the next road (450m).

⑤ Walk along the road R to the bend (200m). Immediately after the house take the footpath L then follow the farm track down over the motorway to fields (400m). Stay ahead on the path between fields (150m) then along the R edge of the field to the road (200m).

⑥ Walk up the road R to the ***Winchfield Inn*** (250m) and on past Winchfield Station to the T-junction (400m).

⑦ Go L briefly (70m) then take the footpath R next to the **railway** fence and cutting (London-Southampton line)(450m). Follow the steps down under the M3 and up the other side (150m). ✪

⑧ Go L briefly on the hard track (50m) then take the track R (60m). Don't enter the field but bear L through the trees (100m) then turn R on the path between fields soon passing a **pillbox** L (100m). Keep on down. Watch out for side paths L & R (500m) then one L (100m) then the one you want, R (100m).

⑨ Take the R path over the corner of the the field (150m). Cross the dual carriageway slightly R and continue on the footpath R of the gas regulator site and up the R edge of the field. Stay ahead to the next road (900m) then go L to the side road at the corner of the tree-covered West Green (200m). ❀

⑩ Turn R into the trees on the downhill path (250m). At the wide causeway path go R, joining the road at Dutch House (350m). Carry on (R) along the road, round the L bend to the R bend (400m) then take the footpath L of the drive of Inholmes Court to the end of the field (100m). ✷

⑪ Cross into the L field opposite and turn L along the hedge (60m). At the large field go up the L edge (300m), R along the top to the stile (120m) then L up the edge of the next field (250m). Exit past the house (50m) and go L on the lane. Watch out for a path R (60m).

⑫ Cut through the wood to the main road (200m). Cross to the footpath, slightly R (30m), and stay ahead on it through heath to the start of a concrete track (300m).

⑬ Follow the main path (300m). At the next 5-way path junction stay on the main path slightly L and descend through the wood then between houses (500m).

⑭ Go R on the lane to the main road (80m). Follow the side road opposite to the pond (200m).

24 The Blackwater, Farley Hill and New Mill

About 9½ km/6 miles with an extension via Riseley Mill of 1¼ km/¾ mile and a short cut of 1½ km/1 mile. Pine plantations, heath, farmland and quiet country lanes. OS maps 1:25000 159 Reading, 1:50000 175 Reading.

Start from the car park at Bramshill Common Wood, SU 760 613, 1 mile from Eversley crossroads beside the Heckfield road.

Linking walks
1✿ 25☆ 27✡

The Fox & Hounds
☎0118 973 6201

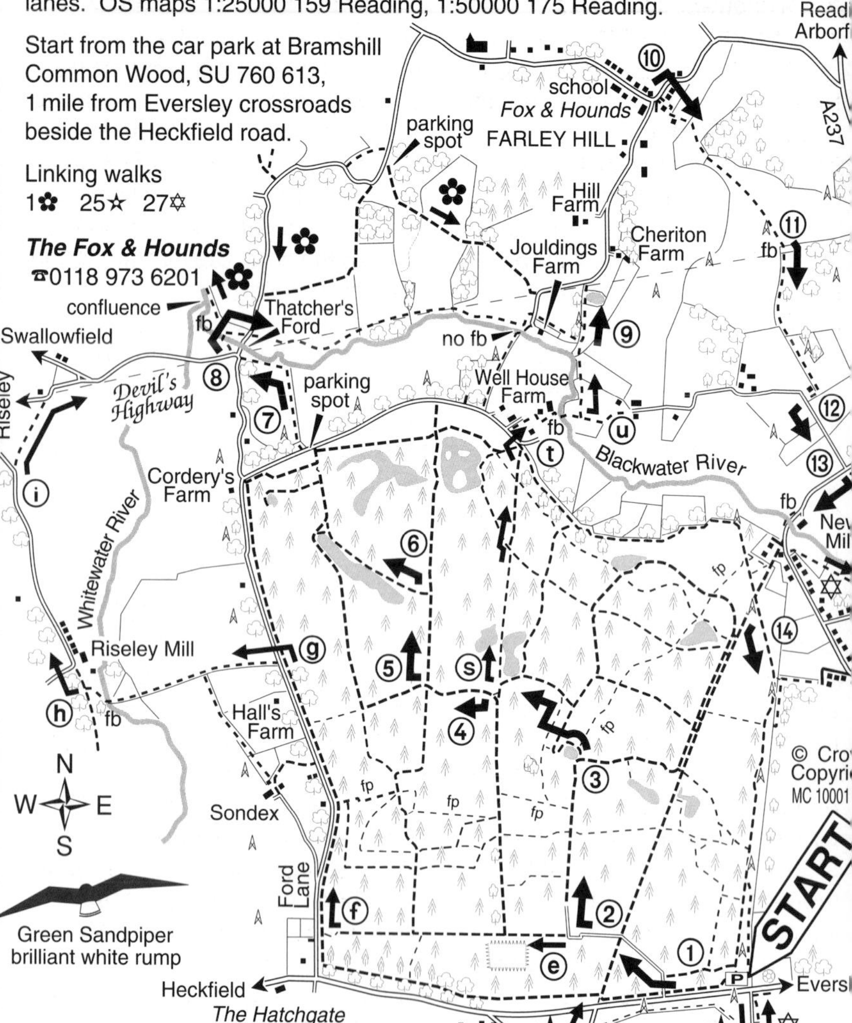

☆① From the Bramshill Common Wood car park, go along the track near the road (300m) and turn R on the concrete forest track. Follow it round L bends to a R bend (500m). ⓔ *Extension 1 km/¾ mile: Stay on the track ahead to the lane (800m).* ⓕ *Go R on the forest track beside the lane, past a thatched cottage L (450m), another house (100m) and Hall's Farm in the trees (250m).* ⓖ *After Hall's Farm (150m), watch out for the bridleway L between the fields and follow it to the end, after the Whitewater River (700m).* ⓗ *Turn R on the track to the road near* **Riseley Mill** *(80m). Continue ahead on the winding lane (750m).*

ⓘ *At the 2nd L curve diverge R on the path between fields (300m) then go R along the next lane, over the Whitewater River (600m) to the road bend and ford (150m).* ➔⑧

② Turn R and continue ahead at the end of the concrete to the bend at the pond (600m).

③ Take the side track L round the pond (150m). Just round the U-bend, exit L to the smaller path (30m) and follow it R to the next track (200m). Go L to the L bend just after the next pond (200m).

ⓢ *Short cut saving 1½ km/1 mile: Take the horse track R (N) near the pond (450m). Slightly L at the cross path (20m), continue in the same direction to the lane (300m).*

ⓣ *Go along the lane L (80m) and take the footpath R of the tarmac drive of Well House Farm. The path zigzags around the farm and over the Blackwater River (250m).*

ⓤ *Soon after the river (50m) enter the field L. Go straight across to the corner (120m) and along the L edge of the next field into the thin end of the 3rd (100m). Don't pass into the next field but turn R.* ➔⑨

④ Go round the L bend (40m) and turn R (W) along the next track to the cross track (300m).

⑤ Walk down the track R (300m), Farley Hill is visible ahead.

⑥ Turn L along the curving side track (450m). After the long pond stay ahead to the end of the track (200m) then on the small path and another track to the lane (100m).

⑦ Along the lane L (40m) take the footpath R through the trees and along the R edge of the field to the end (300m) then L along the river to the lane (150m). Turn R.

The **Devil's Highway** crossed the Blackwater at Thatcher's Ford. The confluence with the Whitewater is at the end of the next field, downstream.

⑧ Facing the ford, take the path L through the field and cross the footbridge (70m). ✿ Turn R back to the lane (100m). Stay ahead from field to field, along the bottom edge near the river, to the next lane at Jouldings Farm (1000m). Keep on through the next field (150m) but in the next field turn L.

⑨ Go up the L edge, past the pond, to the lane (200m). Walk up the lane R to the ***Fox & Hounds*** in Farley Hill (650m).

⑩ Turn R on the road (30m). After two drives R, take the narrow path R between gardens. Turn R across the end of the garden then go L down between fences to the field (150m). Cross slightly R to the corner of the wood (100m) and go down the edge of the field next to the wood (50m). In the next field don't follow the edge but go down the middle of the narrow part then aim for the nearest pylon and the corner of the wood (550m).

⑪ Cross the footbridge and follow the R edge of the wood (150m). Stay at the R edge along the fields until past the house (500m).

⑫ Join the lane (50m) and follow it L to the T-junction (300m).

⑬ Turn R on the lane to **New Mill** and cross the river (300m). ✡ After the ford (50m) and before the bend in the lane turn R along the straight track, past houses and fields to the oblique heath cross track (200m).

⑭ Bear L and stay on the track near the L boundary all the way to the car park (1400m).

25 Around Bramshill Park Pale

About 10 km/6¼ miles with a 1 km/¾ mile extension; deciduous wood and pine plantations. Dry in winter. OS maps 1:25000 144 + 159, 1:50000 186 Aldershot.

Linking walks 21★ 22❖ 24☆ 26☆ 27✷ 29✳

Start from a parking spot in Hare's Lane near Hartley Wintney, SU 770 578, or at the roadside in Plough Lane, SU 754 610, near the Evrsley-Heckfield road.

The Shoulder of Mutton ☎ 0118 932 6272 ***The Hatchgate*** ☎ 0118 932 6666
White Lion Tea Rooms ☎ 01252 844000

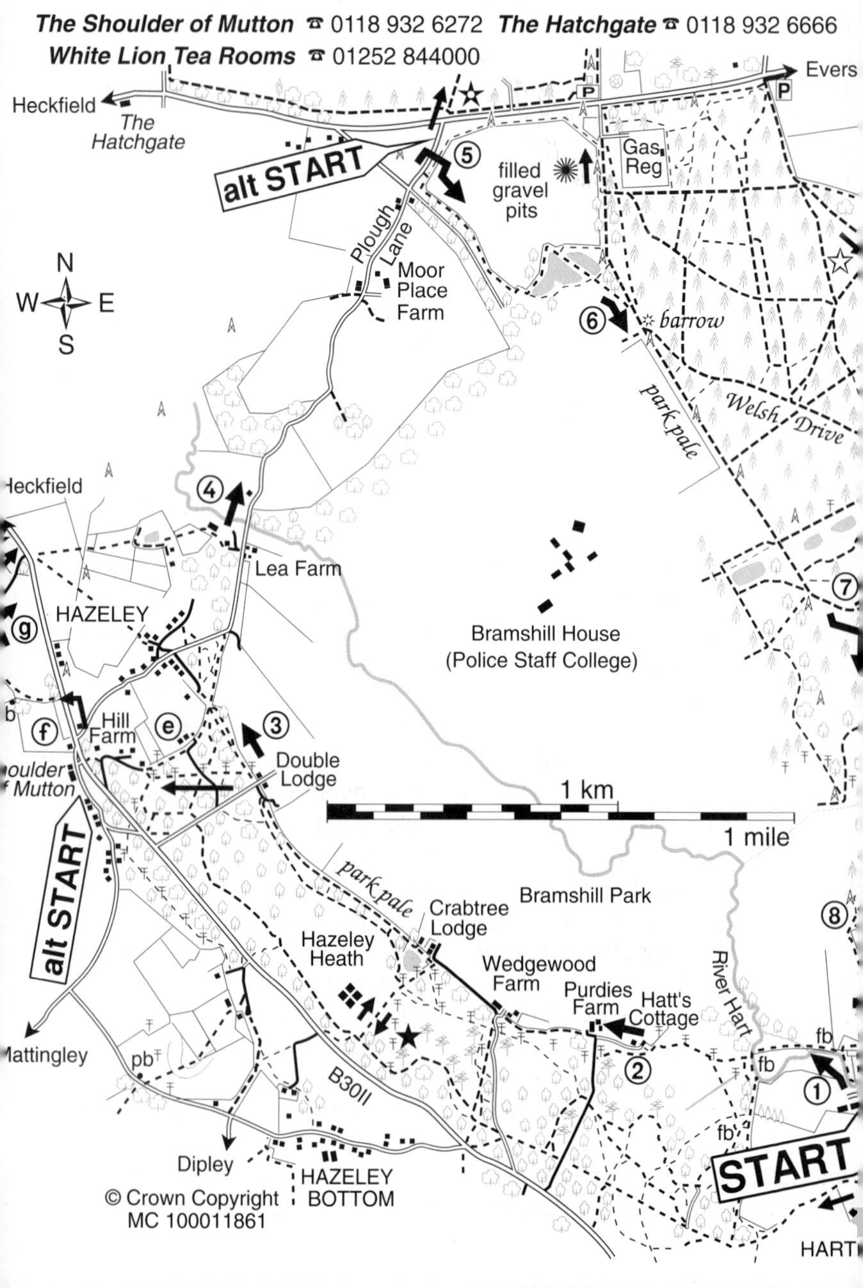

❖① From Hares Lane junction go along the lane away from the main road (200m). At the bend, cross the footbridge R then go through the paddocks along the bank of the **River** Hart and over a stream (150m). Carry on to the next river footbridge (200m). Follow the path over a ditch L then out of the trees (50m) and along the bottom of the heath, disregarding side paths L up the slope. Pass through more trees to Hatt's Cottage (300m).

② Go up the tarmac drive to the farm (200m). Stay ahead beside the **park pale** of **Bramshill** to the next farm (350m), then Crabtree Lodge (300m). ★ Go on past the house, still beside the park pale, to the Double Lodge (850m).

*ⓔ Extra 1 km/¾ mile via the **Shoulder of Mutton**: Just after the drive (60m) bear L up the path with the power cables (200m), over a track to the top (200m) then R to the house (30m). Go up the drive to the U-bend on top (200m). Just after Hill Farm, take the footpath R down to the road (50m) and pub.*

ⓕ Go R along the R verge of the main road (300m). Before the top of the rise take the footpath L along the fence curving R down the large field (550m).

ⓖ Go R on the track to the road (300m) and up the field opposite aiming 100m L of the nearest pylon (200m). Follow the stiles over to the clump of trees L of the house (200m). Beyond the pond take the path slightly L down into the trees to a long building (100m). Go R beside it and on to the road at Lea Farm (100m). Turn L. ➧④

③ Stay at the Bramshill boundary (300m), round the end R and down (250m), continuing on the lane to Lea Farm (700m).

④ Stay on the lane which crosses the River Hart (80m) then winds, eventually up to Moor Place Farm (900m) and down past the next lane junction (400m). ☆

⑤ After the junction (60m) take the path R into **Bramshill Forest** (20m). Go R along the fence (50m), L round the corner and on (500m). When fence and path next bend L, stay ahead beside the flooded gravel pit L (250m). Bear R on the path from between the pits to the forest track at the power lines and Bronze Age barrow (200m). ✸✳★

⑥ Follow the wide track up R with the cables (1100m).

⑦ Stay on the track when it curves L away from the cables (200m). Take the next side track R which eventually drops into a valley (700m) then rises to a U-bend round the R shoulder of the next ridge (300m).

⑧ Turn R down the steep track (700m) and R down the cross path to the corner of a field (100m). Stay ahead outside the field (100m) then along the track (200m) then on tarmac to the L bend (100m) then on the track to the river ford and footbridge (120m). The Hares Lane starting point is L along the road (150m).

26 Bramshill Forest

About 9½ km/6 miles with a cut of 1½ km/1mile and extension of 1 km/¾ mile; an intricate route to see the best parts of the forestry plantations. Most of the tracks are not public footpaths but the Forestry Commission has an open access policy. Tracks are closed from time to time for forestry operations. OS maps 1:25000 144+159, 1:50000 175 or 186.

Start from the parking layby, SU 766 614, beside the Heckfield road opposite a side road, a mile from the Glaston Hill crossroads at Eversley.

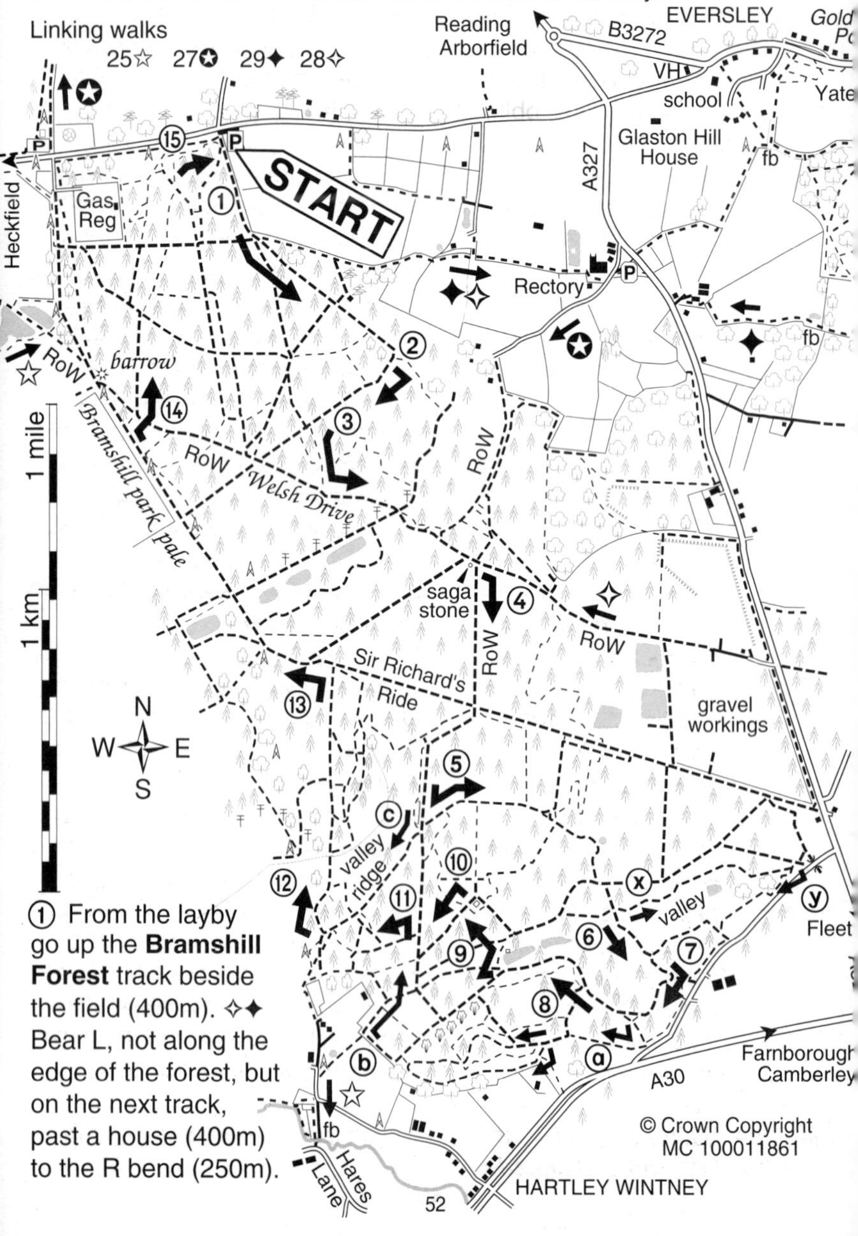

① From the layby go up the **Bramshill Forest** track beside the field (400m). ✧✦ Bear L, not along the edge of the forest, but on the next track, past a house (400m) to the R bend (250m).

② Keep on round the bend and up beside the valley to the side track R on the flat top (400m).

③ Take the path L, opposite the track, round to the next hard track, **Welsh Drive** (350m) and follow it L to the saga stone R (600m).

④ Bear R on the broad track after the stone (500m). Cross another track (Sir Richard's Ride) and go on round a R bend then a L bend (200m). Keep on up to the oblique track junction on top (300m).

ⓒ *A short cut of 1½ km/1 mile: Bear R on the side track along the ridge and descend to the U-bend on the end (500m).* ➜⑫

⑤ Turn back L. Disregard all side tracks and eventually curve round a little valley and up to a T-junction (800m). Slightly L (30m) go down the track opposite (100m).

ⓧ *An extra km/¾ mile: Go L along the valleyside track. Eventually this curves R across the valley and L up to a track junction (650m).*

ⓨ *Turn down R towards the road then follow the winding horse track back near the road to a T-junction (350m). Turn R along the valley side to the major track (300m). Go L up to the curve R (100m).* ➜⑦

⑥ Stay on the track into the valley and up to the R bend (300m).

⑦ Go round the U-curve R and down the winding track (250m).

ⓐ *Alternative - about the same length: Turn L up the first side track (100m). Near the road turn R. Disregard the descending track R (250m) and continue to the side path L (80m). Either take the path L which skirts round the S brow of the ridge (500m) or go on to the track bend (100m) and ahead round the N brow of the ridge (400m). At the end of the ridge drop to the track (50m) and carry on ahead outside the field (200m).*

ⓑ *Go round the corner of the forest and on to the next track junction (200m). Bear L to the steep side track R (100m). Just after it (70m) turn L.* ➜⑪

⑧ Stay on the track down to the fork after the 2nd pond R (700m).

⑨ Just into the R track (20m), take the side path R over a culvert and up past buildings to the next track (100m). Slightly R turn back L up the steep side track (150m).

⑩ Go round the L bend on top and down to the T-junction (300m). Turn R (70m) and take the next L.

⑪ Follow the horse track round the flank of the hill. Stay ahead curving R up to the track bend on the shoulder of the hill (300m). ☆

⑫ Go down round the U bend, ignoring side tracks from it. Cross the little brook (250m) and stay ahead up to the **plateau** and to the T-junction (600m). Turn L.

⑬ Follow the track round 2 curves R (200m) then straight (900m). ✪ 100m before the end of the field L watch out for the small path R halfway between the pylons.

⑭ Cut through to the next track, Welsh Drive (60m). Continue on the other side soon descending beside a little valley R (350m). At the next cross track stay ahead either on the little path 3m R or on the track 50m L, to the next cross track (250m). Still ahead, go down almost to the road (250m).

⑯ Turn R along under the power cables to the parking area (250m).

27 Eversley and New Mill

About 8 km/5 miles or shorter by ¾ km/½ mile, through fields and forestry plantations; half shady. OS maps: 1:2500 159 Reading, 1:50000 175 or 186.

Linking walks 6❃ 24✡ 25✷ 26✪ 28❀ 29✾

Start from the green at Eversley Church, SU 780 609, or the roadside forest car park, SU 760 613 on the Eversley-Heckfield road under power lines.

The White Hart ☎ 0118 973 2817 ***The Tally Ho*** ☎ 0118 973 2134

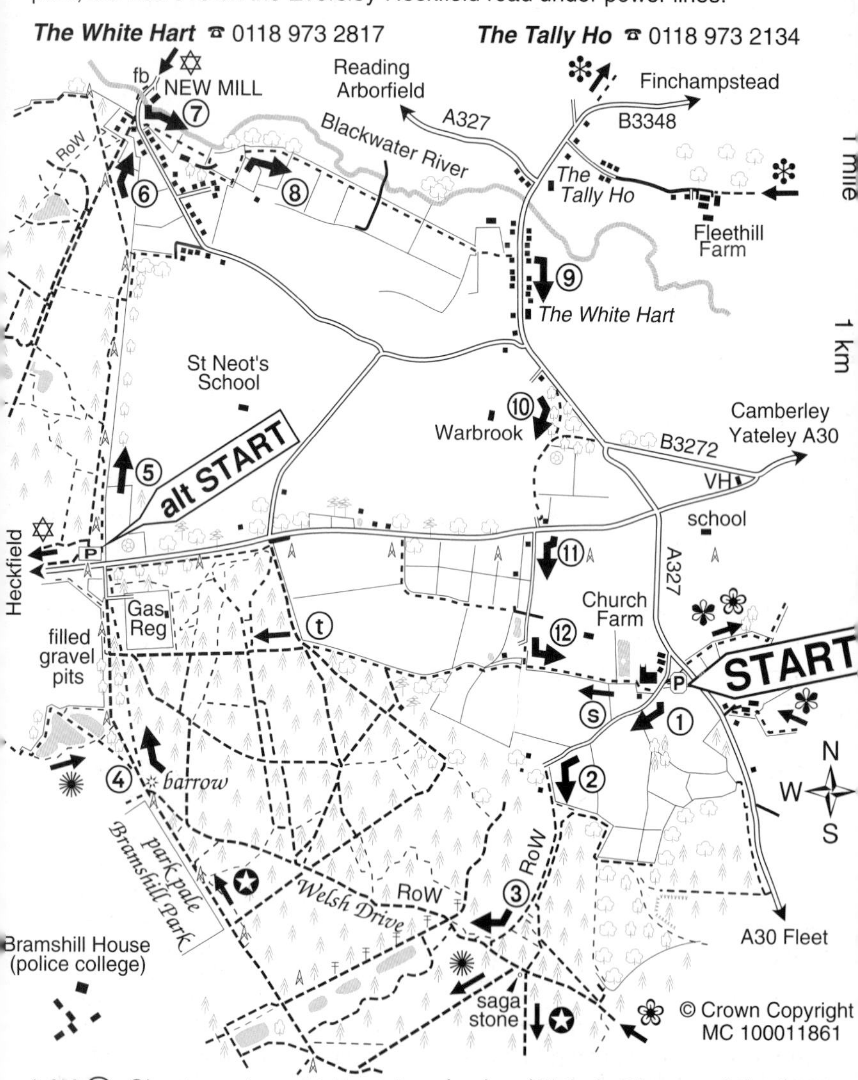

✾✪❀Ⓢ *Short version: At Eversley Church, go through the churchyard round the tower (100m) and out on the path under trees to the fields (50m). Carry on beside the L hedge (300m). Disregard the footpath R after the first field and stay ahead between fields to the corner of the wood (200m) then along the edge of the wood (600m).*

ⓣ *At the end of the fields R take the track most nearly ahead. Disregard lots of side tracks. Continue to the boundary track at the power cables (700m) then down R and over the road (300m).* ➧⑤

① Longer version: From **Eversley** Church walk along the lane past the church and rectory (500m).

② Inside the forest gateway turn L up the bridleway outside the field. Disregard branch paths L and go on to a T-junction (750m). ✵✪

③ Turn R along the wide track, **Welsh Drive**, and disregard all side turns until the T-junction at power lines and a barrow (1300m).

④ Go R briefly on the boundary track (40m) then diverge R on the footpath and stay ahead, down past the **gas regulation station** to the road (700m). Cross.

⑤ From the car park follow the track and power lines away from the road along the E boundary of Bramshill Common Wood (1000m) ✡ and round a slight bend to the oblique cross track (400m)

⑥ Bear R on the hard track. Pass out through the boundary to the road at **New Mill** (250m) and L to the Blackwater **River** (50m). ✡

⑦ Return along the road from the ford (70m). Just round the bend after the track, join the footpath L through the trees. Walk along the middle of the fields R past the large barn (200m) then turn R on the path between fields (30m). Carry on in the original direction through the trees and between fields (120m) then turn L into the field and follow the edge to the wooded end (100m).

⑧ Cross the footbridge to the side field R and follow the edge of the wood then go on between fields to Eversley, joining the road beside Baker's Farmhouse (900m). ❇

⑨ Walk R along the pavement past the ***White Hart***, Warbrook Lane and the drive of the house, **Warbrook** (400m).

⑩ After the drive (70m), diverge R on the footpath. Stay ahead on the track to the next road (500m).

⑪ Cross slightly R and go along the drive (400m). When it bends R to the last house, continue ahead on the short footpath (60m).

⑫ Turn into the field L and follow the hedge all the way to the end (300m) then go on through the trees and churchyard (150m).

The **sarsen** under the trapdoor may indicate Eversley Church was planted on a pre-Christian religious site. Bede wrote that the pope sent Augustine a message in 610 to take over temples. Sarsens are boulders from the Barton Beds left on the surface when the soft sands are eroded. They occur on the chalkland of Wiltshire (greywethers) suggesting it was formely covered by Tertiary Sands. It happens that sarsen districts have poor supplies of building stone so they have all been put to use as standing stones, henges, boundary marks, church foundations, etc.

The Forestry Commission has an open access policy for walkers but sections have to be closed temporarily for logging and planting operations. Small paths may suddenly become wide deep-rutted tracks which after a few years fade away. The Commission was set up after World War I, in 1919, to organise the strategic supply of timber. It provides policy, advice and grants but also has commercial and research divisions. The commercial arm has responsibility for educational and recreational uses which includes the provision of footpaths.

28 Eversley Church, Up Green & Castle Bottom

About 8 km/5 miles with a shorter version partly without paths of 6½ km/ 4miles. Through farmland, heath, woods and Bramshill Forest. OS maps 1:25000 159 Reading + 144 Basingstoke, 1:50000 186 Aldershot or 175 Reading.

Start from the green at Eversley Church, SU 780 609.

Linking walks 25✪ 26✧ 27❀ 29✸ 30✪

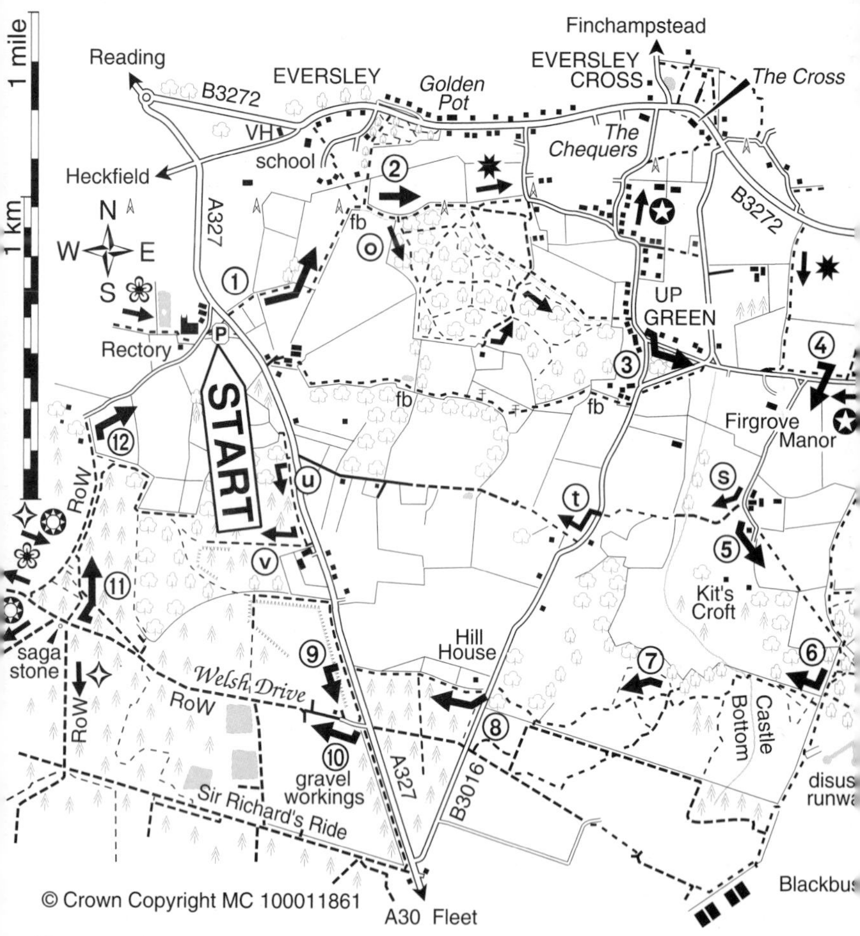

① At **Eversley** Church, cross the main road from the middle of the green to the footpath through the fields (100m). Stay ahead beside L fences until you meet a hedge (300m) then go L along the hedge (300m) round the end R to the next field (40m) and on to the corner of the wood R (100m). ✸✪

② Either stay on the path around outside the edge of the wood to the houses and road (1000m) or ⓞ at bluebell time cross into the wood and follow paths near the R edge round to the house (600m) then, via the vehicle track, return (L) to the edge of the wood (300m) and follow it R to the end (500m).

③ Go R past **Martineau** Cottages to the road fork (70m) and bear L on the lane to the crossroads (200m). Stay ahead up to the layby opposite the gateway of **Firgrove Manor** (200m) then follow the path L of the road (150m).

④ Go R on the next side lane to the bend at Firgrove Farm (450m).

ⓢ *Shorter version (rough in parts): Take the track R down into the valley (200m) and continue on the path up to the next road (300m).*

ⓣ *Walk up the road (100m) and take the path R outside the top of the field. Stay ahead to the next road, the path becoming a track then a farm drive (1000m).*

ⓤ *At the end cross the main road into the trees and make your way L below the road (350m).*

ⓥ *At the warehouses, turn away from the road, along the disused forestry track (350m). When the track ends, bear R through the trees down to the edge of the fields then follow the horse track outside the fields round several corners and ultimately down to the forest gateway and lane (650m).* ➔⑫

⑤ Go round the L bend (100m). When the lane curves up R enter the field L and cut across the top corner to the ridge at the end of the wood (250m). Continue down the next field diagonally to the furthest corner (200m). Exit over the bridge and fork up R. The path soon follows a boundary mound & fence, and joins a track (200m).

⑥ Follow the track briefly (20m) then take the path R downhill near the fence to Castle Bottom (250m). At the bottom turn L over the brook and go up the valleyside (150m).

⑦ Fork R just before the top. Stay ahead on this undulating, winding track over the top and down into a little valley then up through the wood to the road (900m).

⑧ Cross to the path L of Hill House (30m) and carry on under the trees to the next road (450m).

⑨ Cross the road and join the horse track beside it. Go L to the gravel works gate (300m).

⑩ Walk along the gravel works road and continue on the broad forest track, **Welsh Drive**, to the saga stone L (1100m). ✪✧❀

⑪ Take the side track R just before the stone. Go round L & R bends, level then down to the lane (750m).

⑫ Walk along the lane to the church (500m).

Charles Kingsley, 1819-75, was Rector of Eversley. He is remembered for the children's books, *Westward Ho!* and *The Water Babies* but during his life-time was renowned for controversial novels and pamphlets exposing social and public health failings. He claimed to be a Chartist.

The opprobium and admiration which his writings attracted were contrasts characteristic of his life. His religious doubts did not stop him becoming a parson; he swung between bouts of ill health and depression and periods of energetic outdoor pursuits and reform campaigning; he happily left parochial duties for the grand life of rich in-laws but would sit up at night nursing sick parishioners; gypsies and grandees came to his funeral; it could have been at Westminster but he chose Eversley.

He was a fervent natural historian and geologist, unperturbed by Darwin's *Origin of Species* (1859). While Rector he was also at various times tutor to the future Edward VII, Professor of Modern History at Oxford, a canon of Chester and a canon of Westminster.

A life of Charles Kingsley S Chitty 1974

29 Eversley Church and Eversley Cross

About 8½ km/5½ miles or a shortened version of 5½ km/3½ miles, over fields almost level; a bluebell wood; several stiles. OS maps 1:25000 159 Reading + 144 Basingstoke, 1:50000 186 Guildford or 175 Reading.

Start from the green at Eversley Church, SU 780 609, or the layby opposite Firgrove Manor, SU 799 608, or a pub at Eversley Cross, SU 795 616.

Linking walks 6☆ 7★ 8✿ 26✦ 27❃ 28✸ 30☆

The Cross ☎ 0188 973 1126
The Chequers ☎ 0188 973 2116
The Golden Pot ☎ 0188 973 2104

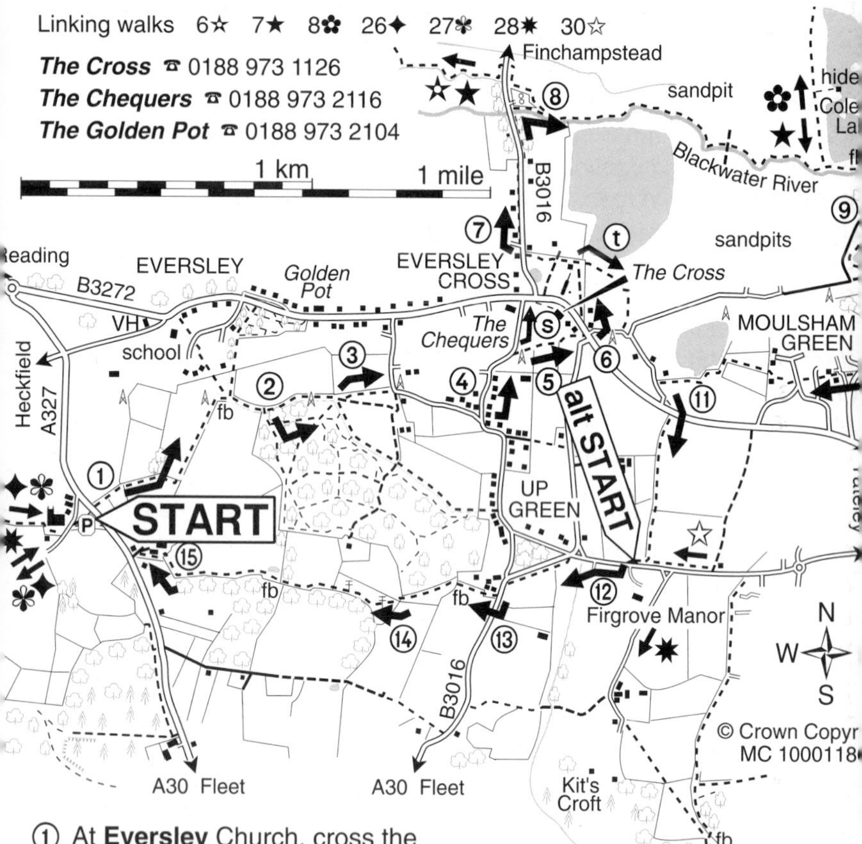

① At **Eversley** Church, cross the main road from the middle of the green to the footpath through the fields (100m). Stay ahead beside L fences until the hedge (300m) then go L along the hedge (300m) and round the end R to the next field (40m). Go on ahead to the corner of the (bluebell) wood R (100m).

② Cross the ditch into the wood (40m) and take the side path L to the 5-way junction (150m). Bear L to the corner of the wood (70m).

③ Follow the footpath beside the fence across the field to the farm (200m). Join the lane at the bend and go R along it to the next junction at the houses of Eversley Cross (400m).

④ Walk along the lane L, round a R bend to a L bend (250m).

Ⓢ *Shorter version: Stay on the lane to the main road at the* ***Chequers*** *(200m). Cross the green to the cricket pavilion (200m).*

ⓣ *Behind the pavilion take the footpath R from the corner round to the lane (300m) then go L to the main road (300m).* ➜⑪

⑤ At the L bend enter the field R and follow the edge of the fields L to the next road (250m).

The ***Cross*** and the ***Chequers*** are L along the road, facing the green.

⑥ Slightly L along the pavement (30m) cross to the green. Make for the furthest corner around the edge or across the middle (400m).

⑦ Follow the road R to the Blackwater **River**; the pavement is on the L (300m) then R (200m); the striking timber framed houses are **Martineau** Cottages. ★☆

⑧ Just over the bridge, drop to the river bank and follow the path between gravel pits past a side path L ✿ (1200m) and part of Colebrook Lake to the footbridge over the river R (100m). ☆

Colebrook Lake is part of Moor Green Lakes Nature Reserve, on gravel pits worked in the 1980s. There are two bird hides for the use of members and more than 200 birds have been seen. The shallows and beaches are profiled to suit the feeding and breeding habits of many waders and swimming birds. Terns and ring plovers nest in summer and there are sightings of rare winter migrants such as red-necked grebe and osprey. The shore vegetation is managed to encourage diversity of land birds and insects. The organisers are the Moor Green Lakes Group which consists of volunteers aided by the extraction company, Semex.

The gravel represents two Ice Age flood plains of the Blackwater River (Terrace 1 & 2 Devensian). Extraction continues in adjacent workings. The gravel bed broadens to a mile here probably indicating a confluence of Ice Age braided streams.

⑨ Cross the river and follow the winding path (either branch) to the road in **Moulsham Green** (800m).

⑩ Turn R (80m). Just after the next side road turn R across the grass (50m). At the next road go R round the bend (20m) then take the footpath L. Carry on in the same line between gardens and over two more roads (250m) then along the L edge of a field (150m). Stay on the footpath which bends L & R to follow the fence round the gravel pit lake to the lane (300m). Turn L to the main road (70m).

⑪ Cross slightly L to the footpath between the fields (30m). Keep on to the next road, opposite **Firgrove Manor** (500m). ✷

⑫ Turn R along the path beside the road to the layby then continue down the road to the junction (150m). Follow the larger road L on the path behind the trees (250m). At the next road junction bear L past the farm buildings (70m).

⑬ Cross the ditch R beside the first field. Carry on into the field and along the R edge (150m) then cross the narrow field to the edge of the wood and follow it L (200m).

⑭ At the corner of the wood bear L, up past an electricity pole, to the trees at the top of the field (100m) and continue along L edges from field to field, over footbridges near the pond (300m) and on to the end of the last field (350m).

⑮ Cross the end of the field to the farm (100m). Outside the field turn L and skirt L of the buildings, to the main drive then exit to the road (100m). Go down the road R to the green at Eversley Church (200m). ✦❃

30 Yateley and the Blackwater River

About 7½ km/4½ miles; with an extension to Eversley Green of 1 km/¾ mile; through Yateley village and past bird reserve gravel pits; a few stiles. OS maps 1:25000 159 Reading, 1:50000 186 Aldershot or 175 Reading.

Start at Horseshoe Lake car park, SU 820 620, or one of the car parks on the village green at Yateley, SU 813 613. Linking walks 6☆ 7★ 8✳ 28✪ 29☆

The Cross at Eversley ☎ 0188 993 1126 ***The Chequers*** ☎ 0188 973 2116
The White Lion ☎ 01252 890840 ***The Dog & Partridge*** ☎ 01252 878382

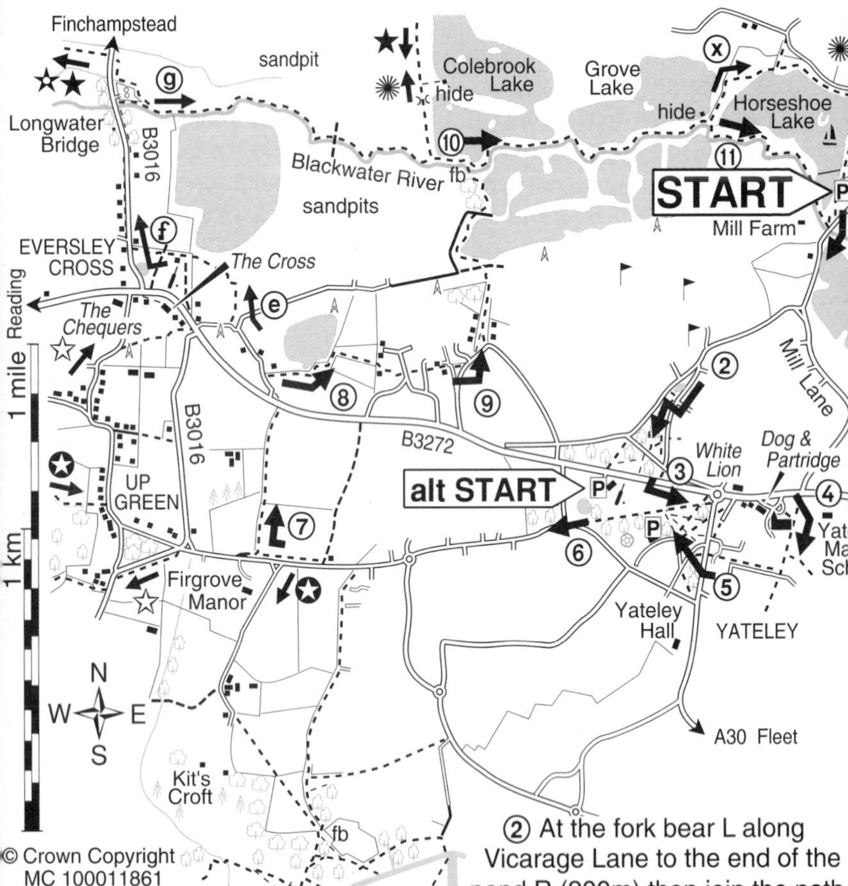

① At the ramblers' car park take the footpath near Horseshoe Lake away from the watersports centre to the Blackwater **River** (100m). Go over the road bridge and along Mill Lane to the junction (200m) then round the R bend along Chandlers Lane (500m).

② At the fork bear L along Vicarage Lane to the end of the pond R (200m) then join the path in the trees between the roads and continue to the end road (300m). Go through the belt of trees ahead and over the main road onto the village green at **Yateley** (100m).

ⓒ *Short cut: Go straight over the grass to the trees (100m) and turn R on the long straight path.* ➜⑥

③ Turn L along the edge of the green towards the old village centre (200m). After the green continue beside the main road passing the ***White Lion*** L (200m).

④ After the ***Dog & Partridge*** bear R to Yateley Church (100m). Go through the churchyard L of the church (50m) and bear R along the fenced path beside Yateley Manor sports field to the next road (150m). Go R along the path R of the road (200m). When the road bends L keep on ahead to the main road (100m).

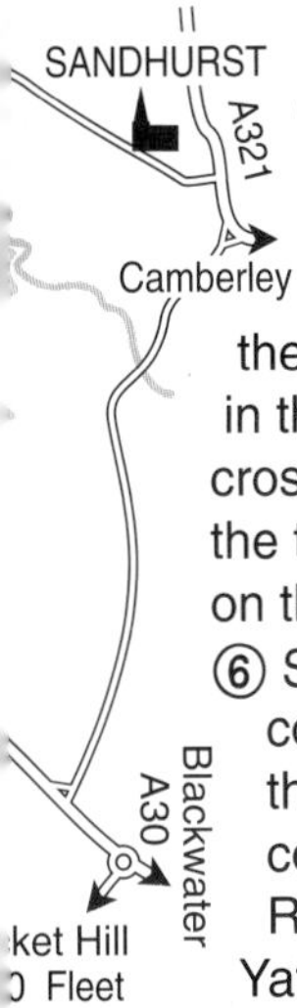

⑤ Diagonally R, cross the road, the verge and the side road to the path through the trees (50m). Continue in the same direction over cross paths to the end of the trees (150m). Turn L on the long straight path.

⑥ Stay on the path to the corner of the green near the pond (250m) then continue along Firgrove Road through part of Yateley (500m), over the roundabout and on between fields (150m). After the thatched cottage continue on the path R of the road until level with **Firgrove Manor** house L (250m). ☆✪

⑦ Cross the fields R along the L edge (500m). The hillside ahead is Finchampstead Ridges. At the end, cross the road slightly L and go on along Fox Lane (100m).

ⓔ *Stay on the lane round L to the junction (250m) and take the footpath R from the L branch. Follow it round to the pavilion in the corner of the cricket green at Eversley Cross (350m). Cross the green, slightly L to the pond (100m). The **Chequers** and The **Cross** are over the main road L.*

ⓕ *Follow the side road away from the village to the river, past the timber framed **Martineau** Cottages L. The pavement is on the L (350m) then R (200m).* ★☆

ⓖ *Over the bridge, drop to the river bank R. Follow the path along the river bank between gravel workings and past a side path L (1200m)* ✸ *to the footbridge R over the river (100m).* ➧⑩

⑧ Just before the first house, Fox Cottage, turn R to the fields. Follow the path along the L fence (250m), across the end of the narrow side field L (50m) then R along the edge of the next field to the houses (150m). Continue along paths between the houses of **Moulsham Green**, over two roads to emerge from a house drive near a triangular grass patch (300m).

⑨ Cross the edge of the grass L to the next road (50m) then go L (50m) and bear L to the footpath through the grassy area between houses. Stay on this path which crosses the powerboat club track (250m) then winds round a gravel pit lake to the river (500m). ✸ Over the footbridge, turn R.

⑩ Stay on the river bank to the side path L at the bird hide (900m).

ⓧ *An extra 400m/¼ mile: Turn L and keep to footpaths near the lake, all the way round to the car park, passing through the water sports centre (1200m).*

⑪ Continue beside the river to the road (600m) then take the footpath back L to the car park (100m).

31 Minley Farm and Yateley Heath Wood

About 7½ km/4¾ miles; mainly through well spaced conifers; undulating; many variants possible. OS maps 1:25000 144 + 145, 1:50000 175 or 186.

Start from the parking spot on Minley roundabout, SU 819 586. Some of the gateways to Yateley Heath Wood have parking spots near the route.

Linking walk 31☆

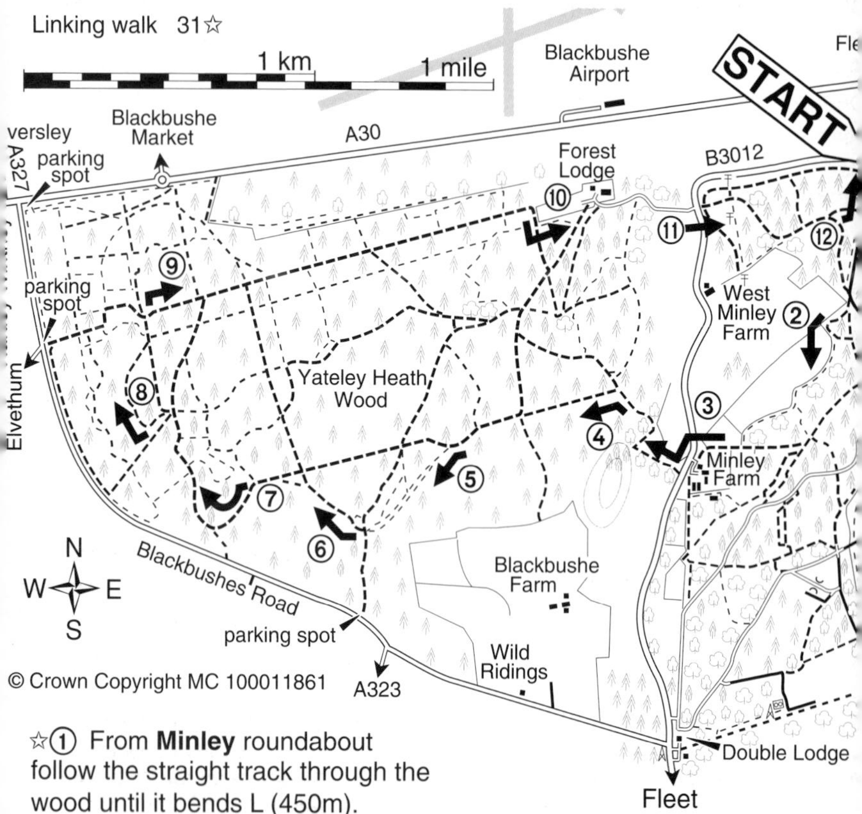

☆① From **Minley** roundabout follow the straight track through the wood until it bends L (450m).

② Bear R on the side track then R again (30m) on the track which curves round L to the field (200m). Follow the fence down the edge of the wood to a track between fields overlooking Minley Farm (600m).

③ Go down the track R and round L to the farm (200m). Walk L along the busy road (60m) then R on the disused forestry track (200m). Go round a R bend to the field (100m) then L up to the major track in Yateley Heath Wood (Forestry Commission) (200m).

④ Take the straight track L (350m) and continue on the wider track which joins from R (150m). The track curves down L then R (150m).

⑤ On the R curve bear L on the path to a track junction (400m).

⑥ Continue on the track ahead curving L & R (200m) then fork L to join the wide track (100m).

⑦ Follow the wide track, down round a L curve past a track L (from the road) (300m) then up round the hillock R to the junction with two side tracks L (600m).

8) Just into the 2nd side track (30m) take the lesser track L up round the valleyside (400m) then walk up the straight track L (80m).

9) Turn R up onto on the wide straight track along the **plateau;** aircraft noise is from **Blackbushe** Airfield. Stay on this track until it bends R near a fence (1300m).

10) Go round the bend (40m) then turn L on the path in the original direction. Follow the fence to the tarmac drive near the house and (ex-)hangar (250m) then follow the winding drive to the road (300m).

11) Cross into Minley Wood. Stay on the track ahead which curves R (off the edge of the plateau) down near a field (350m). Disregard the next side track L (80m) but diverge on the next L (100m) up to the straight track (100m).

12) Go L to the Minley roundabout parking spot (200m).

Yateley Heath Wood is on the same **plateau** as Blackbushe Airport, Yateley Common and Bramshill Forest. The flat surface is uneven where cut by small streams and it is most obvious at the steep edges. A geological investigtion of 1981 suggests it is the 7th terrace of the Blackwater River formed during the Anglian glaciation. The Ice Age had cycles of cold and warm periods. The best understood glaciations are the Devensian, 13-64 000 years BP, Wolstonian 128-347 000, and Anglian, 440-592 000, but there were others before these.

Plateaus are a feature of the area - all attributed to the Blackwater River and cycles of glaciation. The flint of the hard tops was washed out of the chalk hills of the Weald, to lie in great sheets over the surface of the land and wide valley bottoms. At the extremes of glaciation everything was frozen and there was no movement but, during periglacial periods, for thousands of years, the thaws released torrents of water to carry the flints. The tracks are walkable because of the gravel; without it the surface would be soft sand.

During successive periglacials the proto-Blackwater and its tributaries formed valleys within valleys as the waters cut down through the soft Tertiary Sands. After the Ice Age the soft sands continued to be eroded slowly by rainwater but some of the gravel river beds remained in position producing the flat hilltops with steep edges. A neat pattern of symmetrical gravel terraces can no longer be seen because many of the earlier gravel caps have been removed by water action undermining their edges. Interpretation is a three-dimensional jigsaw puzzle using accurate altitude data for the scattered gravel deposits.

There appear to be eleven terraces, more than one per glaciation. The lowest, 1 & 2, are Devensian and do not form plateaus because they lie below the level of the Blackwater River which has lifted itself on alluvium. They are very visible because of the numerous gravel pits along the valley, flooded and made into nature reserves, water sport centres and anglers' lakes. Terrace 11, pre-Anglian, forms the plateau with Bracknell Cæsar's Camp on its edge. Above the eleven, the highest and oldest plateau, at 175m, is the one with Farnham Cæsar's Camp on its edge. It is thought to be much older than the Anglian Glaciation, perhaps 1Ma BP. Its cap is also thicker, up to 6m, and contains larger pebbles.

32 Wyndham's Pool, Hawley Lake and Minley

About 9 km/5½ miles; mainly heath and woods. Most of the route is on military army land which is open to the public but may have army exercises in progress. OS maps 1:25000 145 Guildford, 1:50000 186 Aldershot or 175 Reading.

Start from Yateley Common (Wyndham's Pool) car park, SU 822 596, or the car park beside the A30, SU 832 592, or Hawley Lake car park, SU 839 577.

Linking walks 31☆ 33★

The Crown & Cushion ☎ 01252 545253
The Ely Inn ☎ 01252 860444

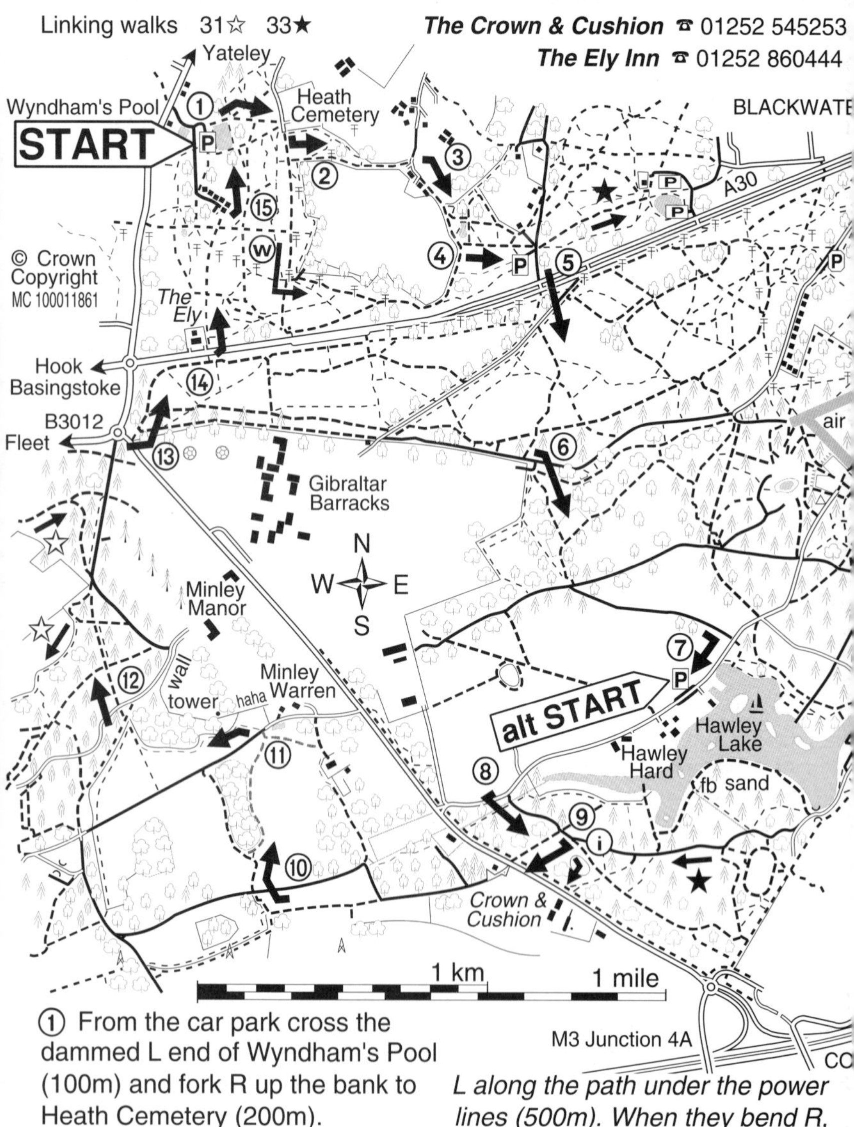

① From the car park cross the dammed L end of Wyndham's Pool (100m) and fork R up the bank to Heath Cemetery (200m).

ⓦ *Winter route to avoid boggy bridleways: Go R on the track from the end of the tarmac (500m) then L along the path under the power lines (500m). When they bend R, follow the track L down round a corner of field (500m). Stay beside the field to the pond (250m).* ➔④

2) Go R briefly (20m) then L along he cemetery fence. Carry on hrough the trees (300m) and join he bridleway, going L between ields to the farm gate (250m).

3) Turn R on the drive (40m) and continue down the bridleway. Stay beside the fields R until past the pond L (300m).

4) Turn away from the field on the uphill stony track and keep on to he 6-way junction near the Yateley Common car park (250m). ★

5) Go R on the track to the road and cross the dual carriageway 150m). Continue on the path into he heath to the tarmac army road 150m). Stay ahead on the track opposite, which curves R to end at he army hard track (400m).

6) Slightly L (30m) take the track R into the wood. Cross the track rom the gate, then bear away from he army fence to the edge of the **plateau** (150m) and drop to the next major track (150m). Go R on he track round down to the hard rack junction (150m). Continue on he track opposite to the tarmac army road (600m).

7) Follow the army road R down past the **Hawley Lake** parking area (200m), Hawley Hard and round a L curve (850m).

8) On the R bend take the curving rack L to the cross track (200m) and go R to the road (200m); but

i) *If visiting the **Crown & Cushion**, stay on the curving track (50m) and ork R (100m) then cross through he beech wood R to the pub (or ake the next side path R) (200m). Return along the tarmac path beside the road (250m).*

⑨ Cross the road and continue on the army road which becomes a track (500m). At the first field R, stay ahead on the track or the path near the edge of the field (400m).

⑩ At the end of the field go R on the track (100m). Cross the hard track and carry on up the winding track (100m). When it curves L, bear R on the faint track around the R edge of the wood (300m). Stay on this track when it diverges from the wood towards the houses of **Minley Warren** (150m), bringing **Minley Manor** into view above.

⑪ Over the hard track, aim for the (water) tower up L in the trees (100m) then follow the edge of the trees L (300m) and round R to the top corner of the field (100m).

⑫ Cross the path at the edge of the wood and continue straight up over the tarmac drive (40m) to the top of the slope (100m).☆ Stay ahead on the plateau to the hard track (350m) and continue on that to the road junction (450m).

⑬ Turn R over the road to the corner of the **Gibraltar Barracks** fence (40m). Take the path to the heath (30m) and turn L on the soft track skirting round the edge (250m). After the end of the curve watch out for the ***Ely Inn*** L (100m).

⑭ Just after it cross the main road L (50m). Take the path outside the R hedge of the inn. Stay ahead to the edge of plateau (200m) and down past power lines to the straight cross track (250m).

⑮ Go R briefly (50m) then bear L down through the trees and keep forking L to the pond (300m). Skirt L of it to the car park (150m).

33 Hawley Woods and Lake

About 7 km/4½ miles with an extension of 3km/1½ miles to Yately Common; woods and heath. Most of the route is on army land; it is open to the public but may have military exercises in progress, sometimes noisy. OS maps 1:25000 145 Guildford, 1:50000 186 Aldershot or 175 Reading.

Start at the car park behind Hawley Memorial Hall, SU 851 593, or at Hawley Sailing Club, SU 839 577. Yateley Common car parks are on the extension.

Crown & Cushion 01252 545253 **Hawley Leisure Centre** bar 01276 35411

Linking walk 32★

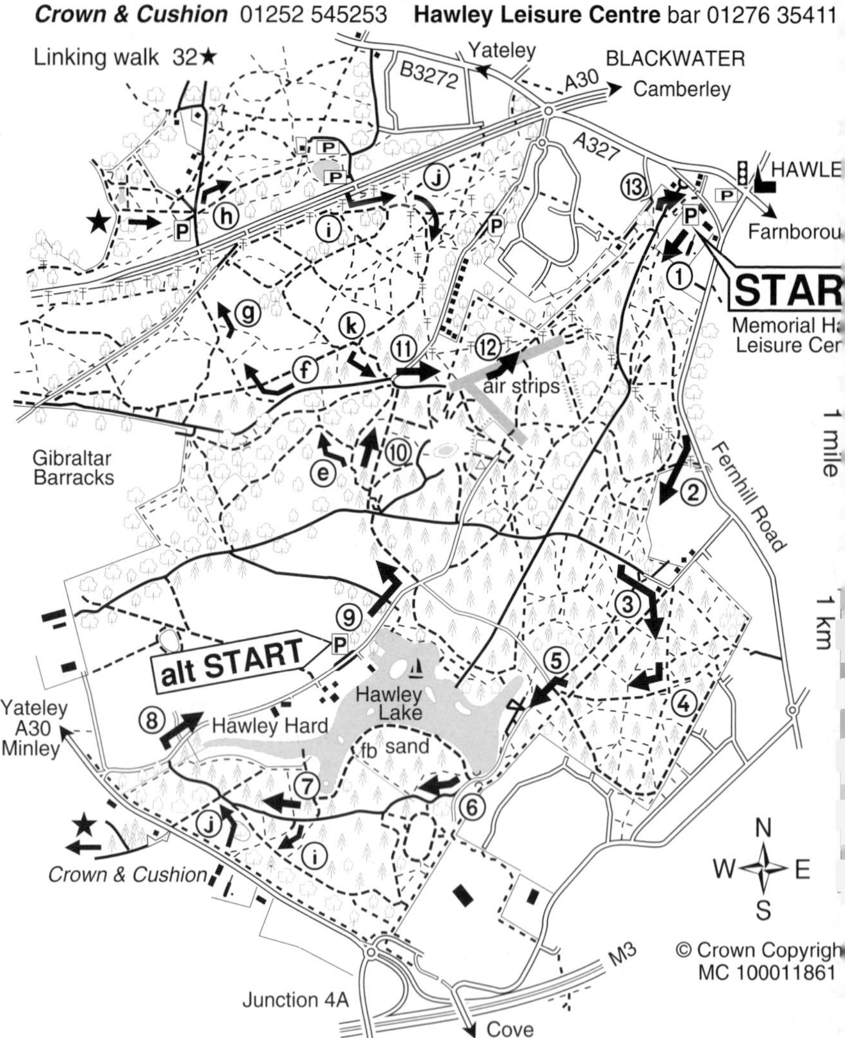

① Behind **Hawley** Memorial Hall climb to the sports field and cross to the far R corner (200m). Carry on through the wood above the valley track (100m) then curve L to a track (100m). Continue on the L arm from the U-bend soon passing close to Fernhill Road (450m).

② When the track swings R near power lines stay on it to the fence

(200m) then bear L on a side path to the edge of the **plateau** (100m) and go straight down (300m).

③ On the track at the bottom, go L to the lodge (200m). Cross the main drive and bear R down through the pine wood to the lowest point (350m).

④ Turn R on the cross track then stay ahead to the tarmac army road (400m).

⑤ From the bend go L on the tarmac, past **Hawley Lake** and over the outlet stream (450m).

⑥ Disregard the track R just after the bridge but bear R at the next wide side track (70m). Go round bends, over a culvert (200m) and on past the side track R (350m).★

ⓘ *If visiting the **Crown & Cushion** After the R track (100m), turn L on the next side track (120m). Cross the clearing and another track to find the path to the pub (100m).*

ⓙ *Afterwards, return straight through the trees (no path) to the 1st cross track (100m) then go L to the tarmac army road (500m).* ➔⑧

⑦ Stay ahead on the main track to the tarmac army road (600m).

⑧ Turn R along the road to the sailing club parking area (850m).

⑨ From the sailing club stay on the tarmac road through the wood up to a tarmac side road R (350m). Opposite the side road, take the track L to the next cross track (300m). Slightly L (40m) go up the track on the other side.

ⓔ *Extension to Yateley Common: Up the track (70m) take the first side track L winding uphill (200m). Turn L with the main track at the next junction. Stay on it up to the apex bend (150m) then branch R up to the next cross track (40m). Slightly R (20m) go on to the parallel hard track (60m).*

ⓕ *Walk L along the hard track (150m) but just round the curve, diverge R on the side path to a cross track (150m). Stay ahead to the curving cross track (200m).*

ⓖ *Turn R to the narrow tarmac army road (200m). Cross it and fork R to the main road (150m). Cross the dual carriageway and continue ahead on the vehicle track to the 6-way junction (100m).*

ⓗ *Opposite the car park track go down the main path R (450m). Continue on the grass, curving R round the pond, and over the car park to the main road (200m).*

ⓘ *Take the little path opposite (30m). Follow the power lines L (150m) then R (100m) to the track.*

ⓙ *Follow the track L, curving R up the slope (look back) and re-cross the power lines on top (300m). Go on along the top of the slope to the next major side track L (300m).*

Visible across the huge Blackwater valley are Wellingtonia Avenue, the Broadmoor rectangle and Bagshot Heath telecommunications tower.

ⓚ *Follow the side track (200m) which curves L across the end of the tarmac army road.* ➔⑪

⑩ Stay on this track to the top of the slope (300m) and turn R.

⑪ Follow the level hard track on the brow of the plateau (200m) and continue along the airstrip (300m).

⑫ Near the end bear L on the hard track which soon descends beside the boundary (700m).

⑬ At the bottom go L on the major track briefly (50m) then take the diverging path R to the road next to the Memorial Hall (150m).

34 Poland Mill and the Basingstoke Canal

About 8 km/5 miles; farmland and canal, almost flat, boggy in winter; lots of stiles; extended version, ½ mile longer; shorter version through Odiham Wood, 1¼ mile shorter. OS maps 1:25000 144 Basingstoke, 1:50000 186 Aldershot.

Start from Broad Oak car park, SU 753 520. On the extended version park at Odiham Wharf car park, SU 747 517, or on the road near the *Waterwitch*.

Linking walks 20✿ 35✪ 36✷ 1✷ 42★

The Waterwitch
☎ 01256 702778

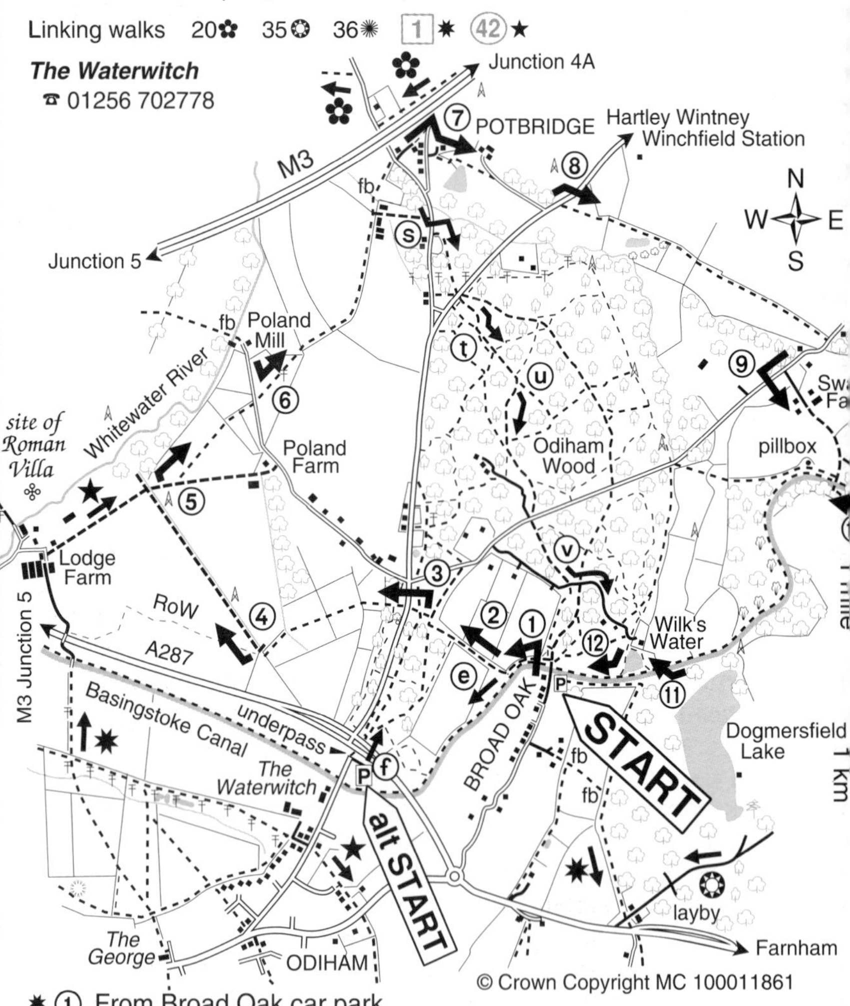

✷ ① From Broad Oak car park cross the **Basingstoke Canal** (60m) and turn L on the first side path down to the towpath (100m).

ⓔ *Extended version, 800m/½ mile longer: Stay on the canal tow path passing under the main road (600m) and* ***Odiham Wharf*** *road bridge (200m). The* ***Waterwitch*** *is just over the bridge.*

★ⓕ *Take the path from the end of the road under the bypass (20m). Disregard side paths and stay ahead through Odiham Common to the end of the trees (500m).* ➜③

② Take the path R of the towpath soon bending away R between fields (450m). At the end of the path turn R, out of the trees (30m).

③ Turn L on the path over the road (between the crossroads and milestone at **Frenchman's Oak**) (50m). Carry on through the trees to the fields (50m) then across the fields from stile to stile (500m).

④ In the last field before the road turn R to the adjacent field. Follow the track (of Lodge Farm) beside the ditch (750m).

⑤ At the cross track turn R but take the path diverging L from it. The right of way is along the L edge of the field initially but the path branches from the track someway from the junction (100m) then runs parallel with the L edge about 100m from it (350m). Enter the next field 100m from the corner and go straight on to the tarmac drive (100m). The route is ahead but go L along the drive, through the garden to see Poland Mill and the Whitewater **River** (200m) then return (200m).

⑥ Cross the next field to the far R corner (250m). Cross the corner of the next field (20m) and go along the R hedge in the next (100m). Over the ditch, carry on ahead up round the R edge of the field and eventually down past Potbridge Farm (500m). Disregard tracks R and stay ahead though the fields to the road (200m). ✿

ⓢ *Shorter version 2km/1¼ mile less through Odiham Wood: Walk along the road R to the first house after the R curve (300m) then skirt round outside of the little field L and keep on to the road (250m).*

ⓣ *Opposite, take the R path soon curving R to a T-junction (150m). Go L, past a cross path (100m) to the next major fork (150m).*

ⓤ *Bear R to the X-junction (150m) then bear L. Keep on to the road (250m). Stay ahead through the wood to the vehicle track (250m).*

ⓥ *Follow the winding track L to the pond (300m). Turn R.* ➧⑫

⑦ Go up the track R of the house opposite (100m). Pass the house at the end and ascend through the trees (60m). At the road go briefly R (70m) and turn L on the first side track (30m). When it bends to the house take the onward side path R (40m) then cross to the adjacent field L (10m). Turn R across the grass past the end of the pond (60m) and ahead on the same line, converging on the drive from the houses. Go on to the road (300m).

⑧ Go L on the road (40m) then enter the field opposite. Aim a bit L across the field for the gate at the far side near a hedge end (250m). Stay ahead at the L edge of the fields to the next road (900m).

⑨ Walk along the road R, round the bends, passing the first house L (200m). Turn L on the track to Swan's Farm. Go up between the buildings and on between fields to the canal (500m). ✪✷

⑩ Don't cross but drop to the towpath R and carry on beside the canal under power cables (1000m) to the end of the fields R (200m).

⑪ After the fields (50m) take the path R (100m).

⑫ Follow the edge of the pond, Wilk's Water back to the canal (100m) and carry on (R) beside it to Broad Oak Bridge (200m).

35 Odiham and Dogmersfield Park

About 8 km/5 miles; towpath and farmland, boggy at ⑧ in rainy seasons; with an extension of 3 km/2 miles across Odiham and a short cut of 1½ km/1 mile. OS maps 1:25000 144 Basingstoke, 1:50000 186 Aldershot.

Start from Odiham Wharf car park, SU 747 517. For the shortest variant use Broad Oak car park, SU 753 520 or the A287 layby, SU 756 512.

Linking walks 34✪ 36✷ 37❄ 1❀ 42✦

The Waterwitch ☎ 01256 702778
The George ☎ 01256 702081
The Bell ☎ 01256 702282

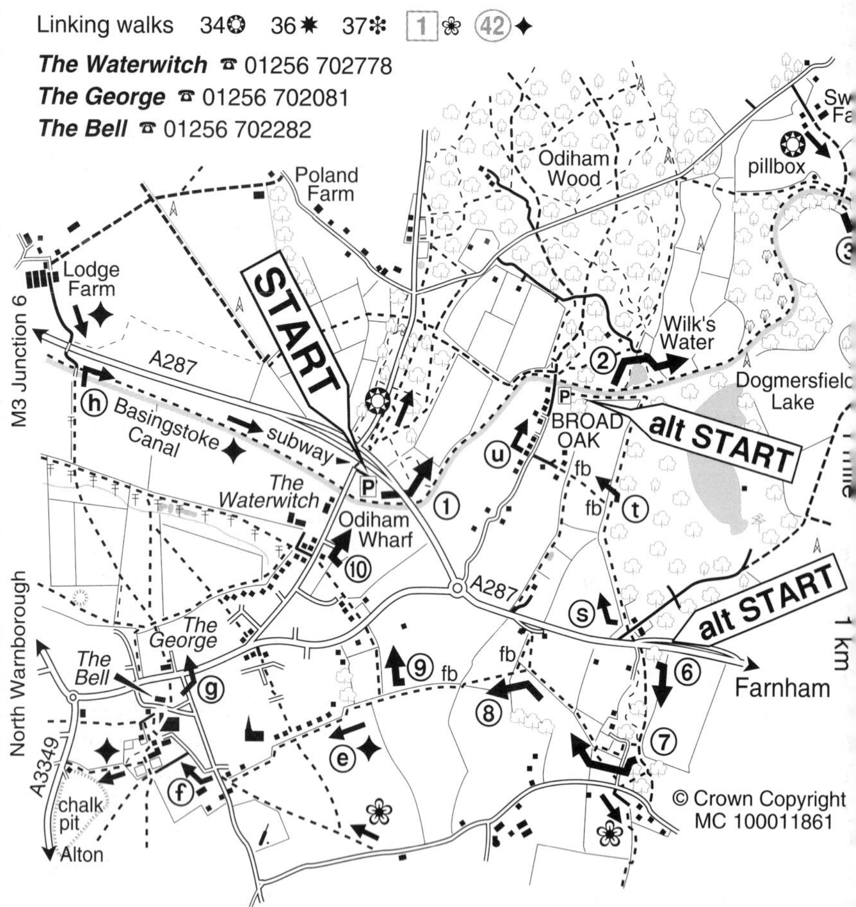

✪① At **Odiham Wharf** car park follow the **Basingstoke Canal** away from the road, under the next road bridge (300m), round L & R curves and past the cart bridge from Broad Oak hamlet (700m).

② After this bridge (220m) take the path L towards the house. Go round the pond, Wilk's Water, and back to the towpath (200m). Carry on (L) along the winding canal to the next bridge (1100m). ✷

③ Cross the canal but carry on beside the cutting (200m) to the track then R past Sprat's Hatch Farm and out on the drive (300m).

④ Round the bend at the start of the road take the footpath R between fields and carry on along the track to the end near **Tundry**

Pond L (500m). ❄ The large house up R is **Dogmersfield Park**.

⑤ Turn back R on the fenced path up the hillside (350m). Join the converging drive and carry on over the ridge. When the drive bends L stay ahead on the track down past Dogmersfield Lake (1000m) then through the wood to the twin lodges (500m).

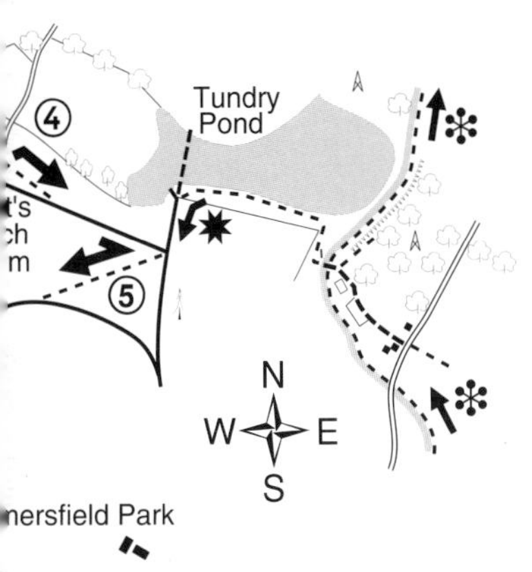

ⓢ *Short cut to Broad Oak car park: Take the path R after the R lodge through the wood watching out for a stile L (400m).*

ⓣ *Cross the field to exit between the nearest houses (150m). Go out to the road (150m) and*

ⓤ *R to the car park (200m).*

⑥ Continue to the main road. Cross and turn back L to the drive of Lothams then go R through the wood. The straight path L of the drive may be boggy. If so walk along the drive to the 1st house and take the winding footpath L, opposite it (300m). ❀

⑦ Watch out for a drive over the R fence and cross it (20m). Follow the footpath L round the paddocks ahead (200m). In the next field continue ahead along the L edge, almost to the far corner (400m).

⑧ Cross the adjacent field L to the next stile (40m) and go over the next converging on the L edge to the stream at the corner (170m). Cross the L boundary and the footbridge and go on along the R hedge (300m).

✦ⓔ *Extension of 3 km/2 miles across Odiham: Stay ahead into the next field and along the R hedge, which bends several times, all the way to the next road (700m).*

ⓕ *A few steps up the road take the side road L & R to the church-yard (200m). The pest house is at the L corner.* ✿ *Cross past the tower of Odiham Church to the road at* the ***Bell***. *Follow the roads R & L to High Street (150m).*

ⓖ *Walk down the drive beside* the ***George***. *Before the arch turn L to the other side of the wall and follow it R to the fields (200m) where several paths meet. Take the onward diagonal path across to the L hedge (200m). Keep on in the same oblique line over the fields (400m). After the electricity poles, continue ahead on the path beside the hedge, over a rise and down to the canal (300m).*

ⓗ *Cross the cart bridge and follow the towpath R to the next road bridge (1000m). Odiham Wharf car park is just after the bridge (100m).*

⑨ Just before the end of the field cross to the adjacent field R and go along the R boundary to the road (250m). Cross and carry on along the footpath ahead between gardens to the next road (300m).

⑩ Walk along the road R past the ***Waterwitch*** and over the canal (200m). Drop to the towpath R and Odiham Wharf car park.

36 Dogmersfield and Tundry Pond

About 8 km/5 miles with an extension of 1 km/¾ mile; almost level throughout; lots of stiles; bad mud after prolonged rain; best at bluebell time; half shady.
OS maps 1:25000 144 Basingstoke, 1:50000 186 Aldershot.

Linking walks 34✷ 35✸ 37✪ 38☆

Start from the canal car park opposite the *Barley Mow*, Winchfield Hurst, SU 777 538. On the extension, Winchfield Church has a car park, SU 767 536.

The Queen's Head ☎ 01252 613531 ***The Barley Mow*** ☎ 01252 617490

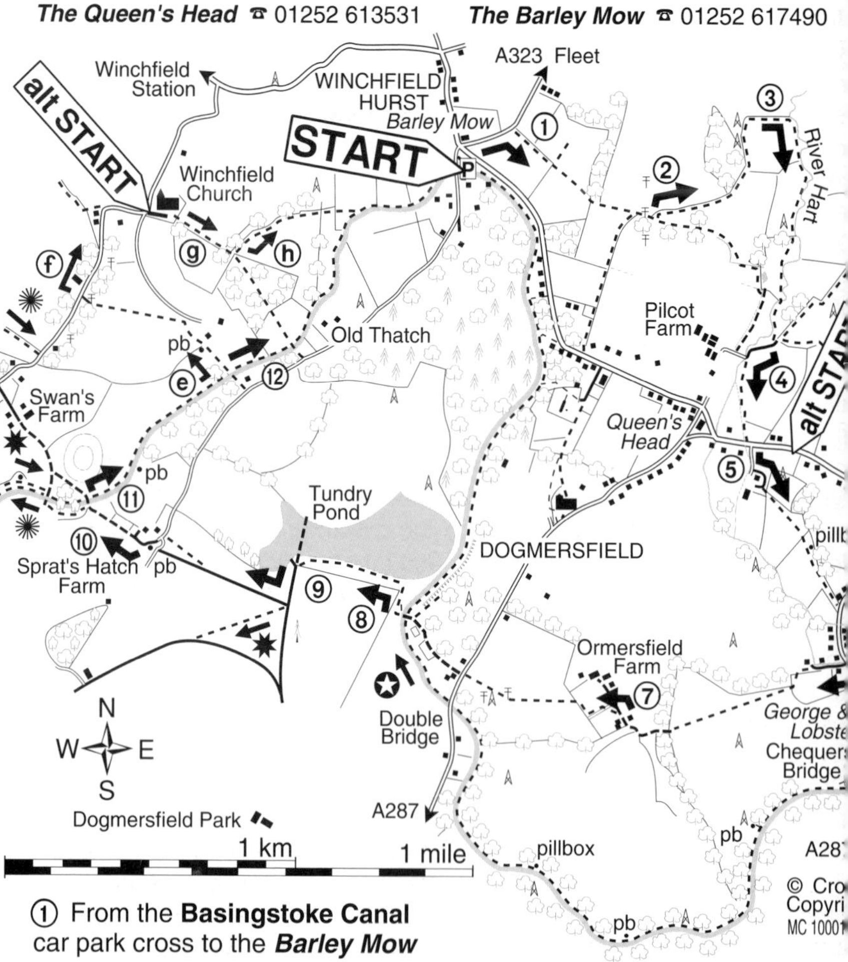

① From the **Basingstoke Canal** car park cross to the ***Barley Mow*** and go along the side road beside the pub (200m). At the bend enter the field R and follow the path across the paddocks to the trees (250m). Go on through the trees past the end of the next field R (150m) and a bit further (50m).

② Turn to the field L and follow the diverging L edge (300m). Bear L round the edge of the wood to the corner after the pylons (300m).

③ Cross the end of the field R (150m) and follow the **River** Hart back along the field and two more o the footbridge over the river 650m). Cross and follow the river o the end of the field (150m). ✪

④ Go R on the track (120m). Don't ross the farm bridge but continue head on the path beside the tream to the road (250m) (The ***Queen's Head*** is 200m R.) Cross lightly L (20m).

⑤ Walk along the drive of Brook-neadow Farm Stables (80m). 3efore the house take the track L ound the garden (70m). From the corner nearest the power cables ake the path through the fields. Diverge very slightly from the L edge to cross into the next field 50m from the corner (200m) and carry on past a **pillbox** (80m) to he far L corner (200m). Walk long the road R (200m). ☆

⑥ After the 2nd bridge turn along he track R, Stroud Lane (150m). Vhen the track bends to the last iouse keep on briefly outside the ield (50m) then into it. Cross the R corner (40m) to the next large field. Go on, diverging slightly from the R edge, aiming between the pylon L and trees R (200m). Carry on over he top and down towards the gap n the trees (and a distant pylon) 250m). Pass through the belt of rees, along the winding cart track and up between houses (200m).

⑦ Just after the first houses take he path L across the corner of the ittle field (20m). Go over more ences, L & R round outside the iext field (120m) then diagonally over the large field towards the vhite house. Sometimes the path goes direct but the right of way is lightly L and bends towards the iouse at the electricity pole before the pylon (400m). Cross the road and go down the path beside the drive then along the track at the edge of the wood, round a L bend and over the canal (300m).

⑧ Turn R beside the next field down to **Tundry Pond** (100m) and go L along the edge (350m). ✷

⑨ Turn L along the track towards **Dogmersfield Park** (150m) then take the level track R between fields (300m) and diverge R on the path to the trees and buildings at Sprat's Hatch Farm (200m).

⑩ Join the lane but turn L on the farm track and go round the bend. Keep on between fields and over the canal bridge (300m).✷

⑪ Descend R to the towpath and keep on beside the canal to the next bridge (Badeley's) (700m).

ⓔ *Extension of 1 km/¾ mile to* **Winchfield Church***: Up on the bridge take the track L. Continue past the large house (Old Rectory) almost to the tarmac drive (250m) then enter the field L and diverge from the R edge across to the gap in the trees (400m).*

ⓕ *Walk along the lane R (300m) and round the R bend to the* church *(150m).*

ⓖ *Go through the churchyard (100m) and take the path, exactly in line from the end of the track, at the R edge of the field (200m) and through the belt of trees (30m).*

ⓗ *At the next fields turn L. Go along the L edge (350m), over a narrow field and straight on to the canal (100m). Go L to the car park just after the next bridge (400m).*

⑫ Stay on the towpath under the next bridge (200m), and the next (900m), to the car park L.

37 Crookham and the Basingstoke Canal

About 9 km/5½ miles; canal towpath and farmland with lots of stiles, flat, mostly shady; with two extensions each of ¾ km/½ mile. OS maps 1:25000 144 Basingstoke, 1:50000 186 Aldershot.

Start from Crookham Wharf car park at Chequers Bridge, SU 791 517. One of the extensions passes a canal car park opposite the *Barley Mow*, SU 778 538.

Linking walks 35❄ 36✪ 38✦

The George & Lobster ☎ 01252 615336 ***The Black Horse*** ☎ 01252 616434
The Queen's Head ☎ 01252 613531 ***The Barley Mow*** ☎ 02521 617490

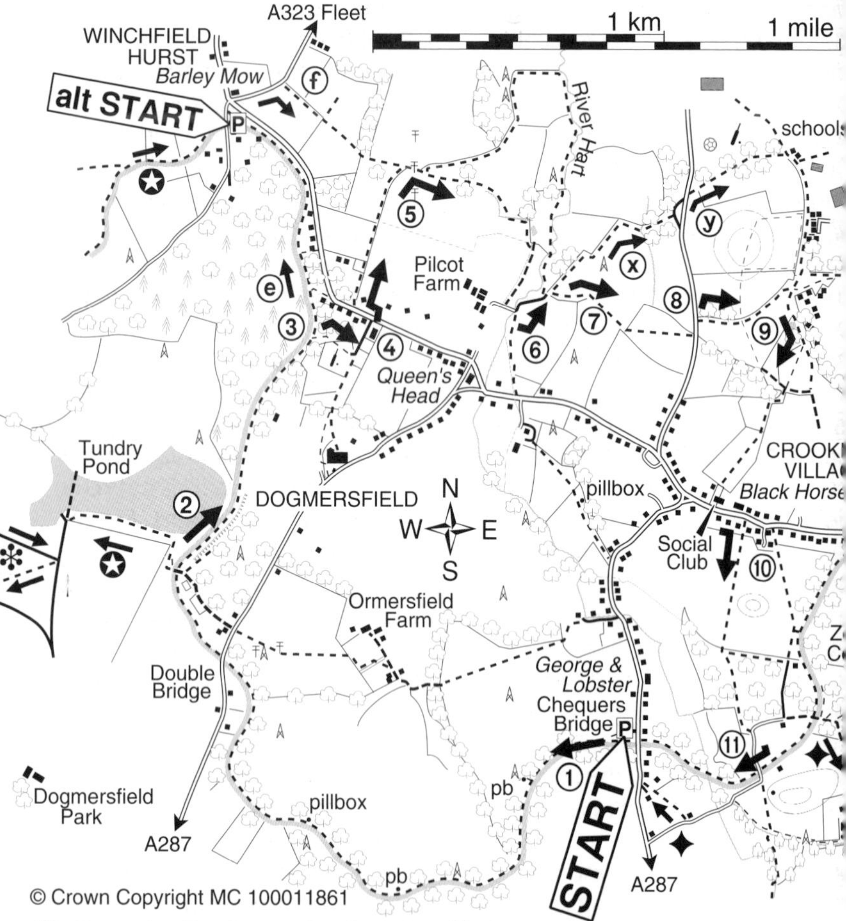

① From the **Basingstoke Canal** car park, join the towpath and walk away from **Chequers Bridge**. Go on to the next bridge (2400m). Pass under it and under the next (Blacksmith's)(350m). ❄✪

② Stay on the canal embankment past Tundry Pond L (400m) into a cutting. Opposite the pines L when the cutting is nearly level with the towpath, watch out for the cricket field R, through the trees (800m).

ⓔ Extension of ¾ km/½ mile to the Barley Mow: Stay on the towpath almost to the next bridge and cross the car park to the pub (950m).

*ⓕ Go along the side road beside the **Barley Mow** (200m). At the bend enter the field R and follow the path across the paddocks to the trees (250m). Go on through the trees to the end of the next field R (150m) and ahead. ➧⑤*

③ Go through the trees, beside a ditch then R into the corner of the cricket field (50m) and across or L round the edge to the exit (150m). Follow the vehicle track out past the school (150m).

④ Go L on the road briefly (60m) then take the path R into the wood (near sewage works). Carry on past the garden to fields (100m) and along the R edge to the next trees (350m). At the end turn R.

⑤ Keep on along the path in the belt of trees (300m). After the trees, continue round the R edge of the field (150m). Just before the next side hedge L, cross the ditch then continue at the L hedge (100m). In the field after the pond follow the farm track R beside the ditch towards Pilcot Farm (300m).

⑥ At the farmyard go L on the concrete track over the **River** Hart (50m) and turn L on the track through the trees into the field ahead (200m).

ⓧ Extension of ¾ km/½ mile: At the end of the track stay ahead near the L edge of the field and R round the end to the wood (400m). Go through the wood (200m) and L on the track to the road (20m).

ⓨ Slightly L (20m) take the path through the trees on the other side Stay on this path round the field with the hillock all the way to the clearing at the edge of the housing estate (900m). Carry on along the path R of the houses. ➧⑨

⑦ Turn R along the hedge (70m). At the hedge-end continue straight up the field to a zigzag in the hedge (150m). Cross the next field to the far L corner and go out to the road (250m).

⑧ A little L (60m) continue in the field opposite outside the hedge of the field with the hillock towards houses (400m). Turn R on the cross path near the houses.

⑨ Stay on the path skirting R of the trees round the houses (Fleet) (200m). At the field after the pond, cross obliquely to the L end of the wood (150m). Cross the boundary track and follow the track round the narrow end of the wood into the next field. Go up the L edge (200m) then diagonally up through the top field and across the club car park to the road in **Crookham** Village (350m). ✦☼

⑩ Walk L along the road past the ***Black Horse*** (100m). Just after the pub watch out for the path between houses R (30m). Follow this path up between fields and down to the wood (450m). Stay ahead through the wood to the tarmac lane (300m). Go R up the lane to the humped Poulter's Bridge over the canal (150m).

⑪ Don't cross but join the towpath and go R beside the canal to the next bridge, Chequers, and the car park (450m). The ***George & Lobster*** is just along the road L from the car park (150m).

38 Crookham Village and Crondall

About 8 km/5 miles with extensions to the village centres; gently undulating farmland with lots of stiles; paths very overgrown in late summer.
OS maps 1:25000 144 Basingstoke +145 Guildford, 1:50000 186 Aldershot.

Start from Chequers Bridge car park at Crookham Village, SU 791 517, or, on the extensions, from a pub or roadside parking spot in one of the villages.

36☆ 37✦ 39✫ 4 ❀ 5 ✧ 6 ✾ 7 ✡

George & Lobster 01252 615336
Black Horse 01252 616434
Hampshire Arms 01252 850418
Plume of Feathers 01252 850245

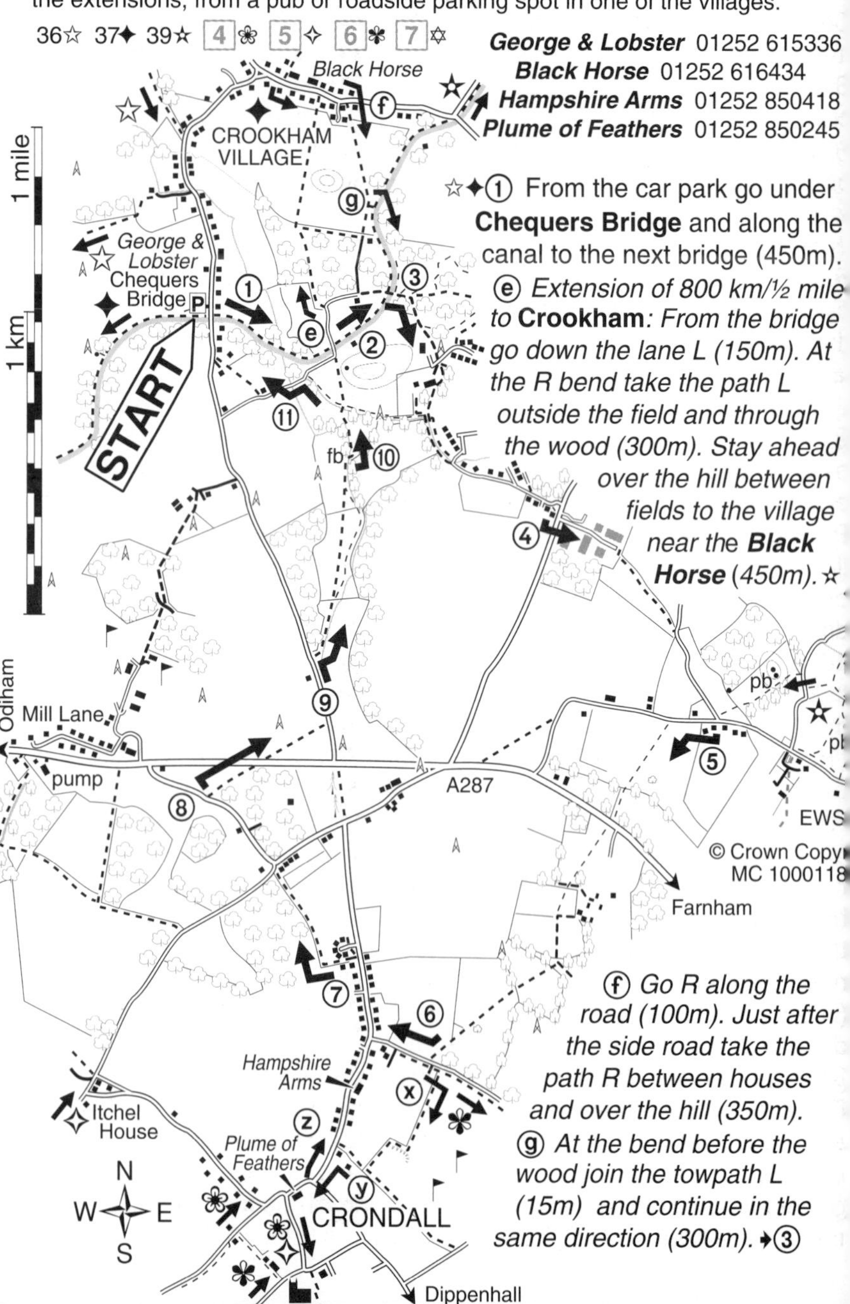

☆✦① From the car park go under **Chequers Bridge** and along the canal to the next bridge (450m).

Ⓔ *Extension of 800 km/½ mile to* ***Crookham****: From the bridge go down the lane L (150m). At the R bend take the path L outside the field and through the wood (300m). Stay ahead over the hill between fields to the village near the* ***Black Horse*** *(450m).* ✫

Ⓕ *Go R along the road (100m). Just after the side road take the path R between houses and over the hill (350m).*

Ⓖ *At the bend before the wood join the towpath L (15m) and continue in the same direction (300m).* ➜③

② Stay on the towpath (350m). ☆

③ At the swing bridge cross to Zebon Copse. Keep to the main track round a R bend (100m) and on between fields (300m). After the tarmac drive of the Community Centre take the path under the trees which bends behind the barn. Stay ahead to the next tarmac crossing (350m). Over the bridge R (20m) carry on as before, now on tarmac, to the road (400m).

④ Cross slightly R and go along the road between the buildings of Redfields Park (200m). At the end carry on along the L edge of the field to the lane (400m). Follow the lane R to the end opposite **Ewshot** Lodge (300m). ✡

⑤ Go R along the lane out of the hamlet (200m). On the rise and curve (50m before the next house R) take the path L straight across the field. Look straight over for the nearest large tree and the top of a distant pylon. Aim R of the pylon or 100m R of the tree then make for the stile (250m). Stay ahead along the hedge to a nasty road crossing (100m). Go straight on over the paddocks from stile to stile, 100m R of the farm (250m). After the hedge cross another paddock then follow the horse track to the next hedge (250m). Just round the bend in the trees, turn R to the next field (30m). Go straight over (120m) and ahead between fields down to the lane (350m). ✾

ⓧ *Extension of 1 km/¾ mile into* ***Crondall****. Join the path opposite, above the lane, and go L past the field entrance (50m). Turn R at the golf course and follow the fence, with a zigzag, to the end (500m).*

ⓨ *At the hedge, go R to the road (120m) and L along the street to the* ***Feathers*** *(300m).* ✧❀

ⓩ Return along the same road but carry on past the field, and the ***Hampshire Arms*** (500m) to the edge of the village (400m). ➔⑦

⑥ Follow the lane R to the village street (250m) and go R to the edge of the village (300m).

⑦ Just before the fields R, turn L on the house drive. Go up between houses to the field (120m) and R along the top edge next to the wood (300m). Stay ahead curving L to the road junction (100m). Go on in the same direction down the road with the wood R (300m).

⑧ At the end of the wood take the path R beside the trees to the main road (200m). Cross on the same oblique line and carry on along the path at the edge of the field (300m). At the next road go L (250m).

⑨ After the house L (50m) take the path R in the fields. Don't cross the stream but go L beside it. The right of way is at the middle of the fields but the path usually follows the stream, converging on the wood at the far side (300m), then the R edge of the fields (400m).

⑩ Between the crossing power lines watch out for a footbridge R under the trees and cross the stream (20m) then turn L beside the trees (100m). When the stream and trees bend L, cross to the end trees and go through the gateway to the next field (70m).

⑪ Follow the L edge (150m) then the lane (150m) After the house go R up the path between wood and field (200m). At the road go R to Chequers Bridge (150m).

39 Fleet, Basingstoke Canal and Ewshot

Longer than usual, about 11½ km/7 miles; the towpath through Fleet and heath gentle inclines. OS maps 1:25000 145 Guildford, 1:50000 186 Aldershot.

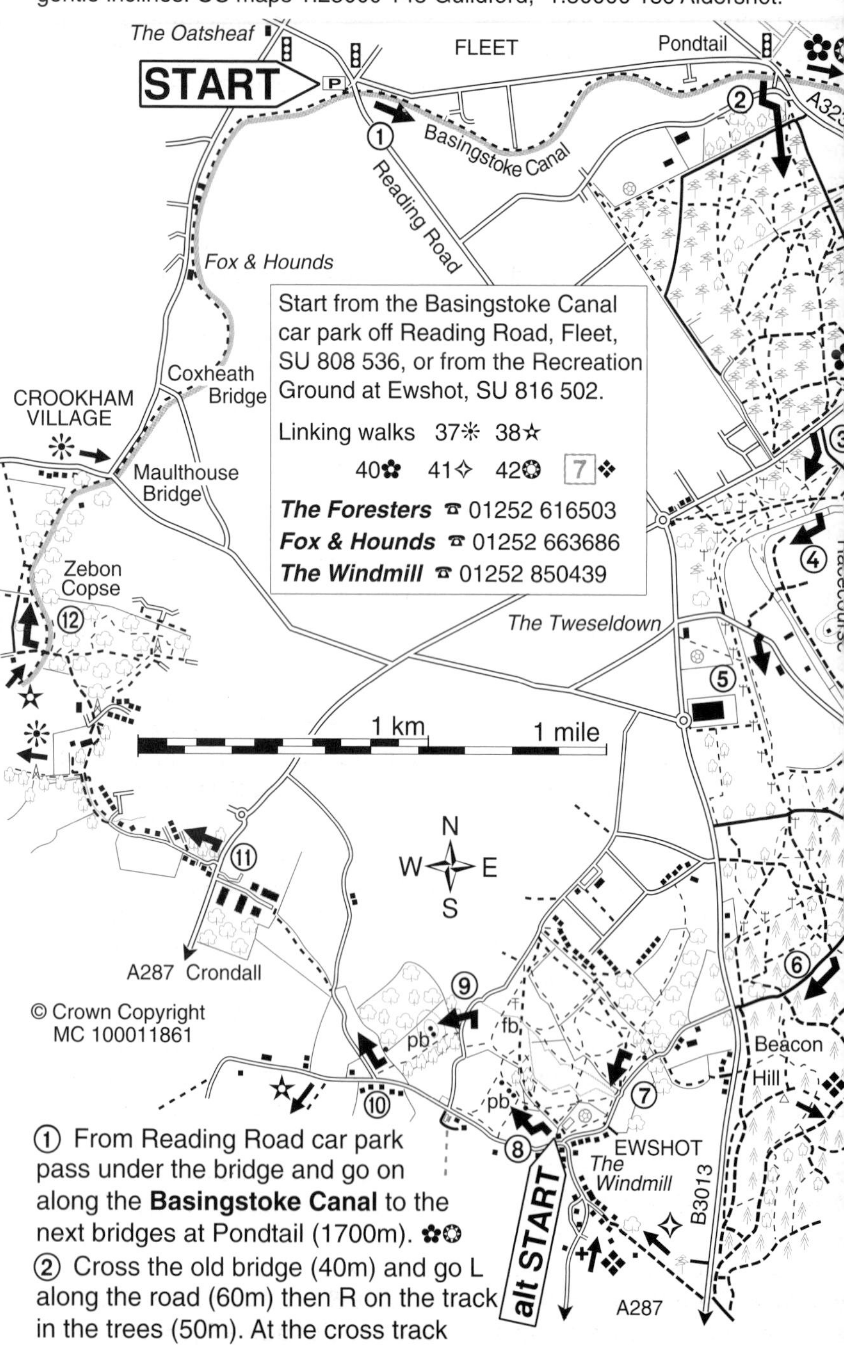

① From Reading Road car park pass under the bridge and go on along the **Basingstoke Canal** to the next bridges at Pondtail (1700m).

② Cross the old bridge (40m) and go L along the road (60m) then R on the track in the trees (50m). At the cross track urn R (20m) then L on the side path (350m). At the cross track after the ditch (40m) take the L path ahead (200m) joining a track o the road (450m). The building 00m L is the ***Foresters***.

3) Go R briefly on the track beside he road (40m) then cross to the rack opposite and walk away from he road (150m). Turn R along the path beside the fence (and near **oil pipeline** marks). Disregard the side paths and carry on into **Tweseldown** Racecourse (200m).

4) Cross the grassy race track and urn R after the hedge. ✧ Follow a horse track near the race track round the bend (250m) and re-cross the race track via the vehicle rack to the road (150m).

5) Cross the road into the field duck through the fence) and go up he R edge. (Outside the field there s a parallel public RoW.) At the end of the field continue on the RoW with power lines to the cross rack (700m) and ahead, R of the power lines to the next cross track 300m). Stay ahead to the next cross track (200m). ❖

6) Turn R and descend to the road fast cars) (450m). Follow Tadpole Lane, opposite, past Beacon Hill Farm (150m) and round the little S-bend (200m).

7) At the **pillbox** R climb the bank and go out into the field (30m) then urn L and follow paths round, near he road, to Ewshot Recreation Ground car park (450m). The ***Windmill*** is 250m up the lane L.

8) From the car park at **Ewshot** ascend beside the L fence (50m) and go on through the next field army land) (100m). Watch out for the first side path L and follow it across the clump of trees, past the pillboxes and round the end of the hill to the hedge (300m). Go down the next field, keeping near the hedge, and out to the lane at the gate in the corner or the hole in the hedge 20m R of it (100m).

⑨ Walk along the lane R (50m) and turn L into the first gateway (army land). Follow the trees up the L edge of the field past the pillboxes on top and down (250m). From the middle of the bottom edge cross the next field to the gateway in the trees opposite, to emerge on the lane near a T-junction (80m). ☆

⑩ Walk down the lane R to the R bend (300m). Go through the field ahead along the R edge. The footpath is blocked by rubble so enter via the gate and skirt round the rubble tip. At the end (400m) exit to the industrial estate and walk along the main drive to the road in Church Crookham (200m).

⑪ Cross slightly R and walk along Watery Lane, opposite, to the bend and bridge (450m). Don't continue on the bridleway unless the stream bed is dry but cross the bridge (20m) to the path L which re-joins the bridleway later (200m). ✳ Go on along the bridleway (200m), over the drive of Velmead Community Centre and ahead at the edge of Zebon Copse to the Basingstoke Canal (300m).

⑫ Over the swing bridge turn R and follow the canal through **Fleet**: under Malthouse Bridge (700m), and Coxheath Bridge (400m) to the ***Fox & Hounds*** (600m) then to Reading Road wharf (950m).

40 Fleet Pond and Velmead Common

About 8 km/5 miles with an extension of 1 km/¾ mile; many short cuts possible; heath and woodland; no stiles, fairly shady; passable in winter. OS maps 1:25000 145 Guildford, 1:50000 186 Aldershot.

Start from the heath car park near *The Foresters*, SU 826 527, or Norris Bridge car park, SU 833 536, or one of the streets adjacent to the pond in Fleet.

Linking walks 39✿ 41❃ 42★ **The Foresters** ☎ 01252 616503

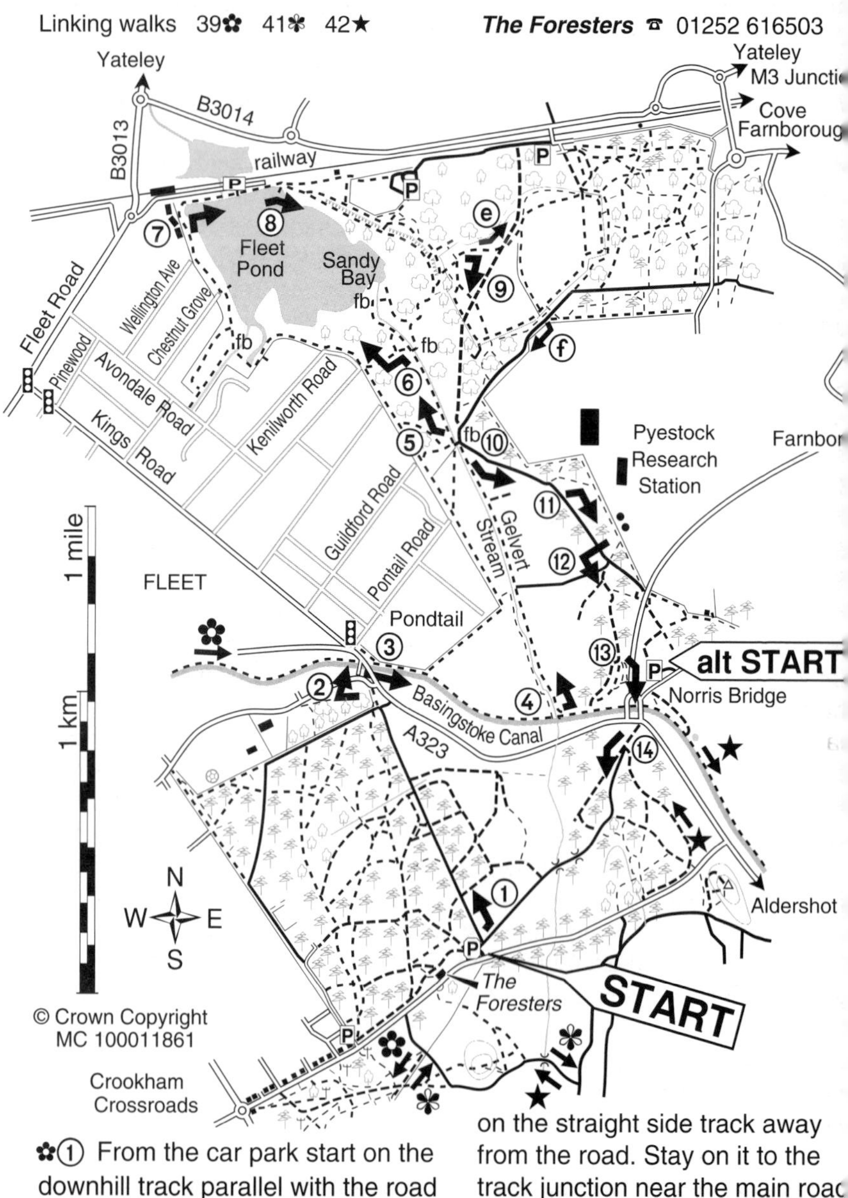

✿① From the car park start on the downhill track parallel with the road but almost immediately (30m) turn L on the straight side track away from the road. Stay on it to the track junction near the main road at the end of the heath (850m).

② Continue on the path ahead to the minor road (70m). Go L to Old Pondtail Bridge and cross (80m).
③ Drop to the towpath R, pass under the main road and carry on beside the **Basingstoke Canal** to the sluices (550m).
④ Cross the overflow weir and turn L down to the Gelvert Stream which emerges from under the canal. Stay on this footpath to the bridge at the junction of several paths and tracks (1100m).
⑤ Cross the stream but carry on beside it (350m).
⑥ Just after the next footbridge turn L to the road (200m). Follow the boundary path R, curving L then round R & L bends and over a footbridge (600m). Stay ahead to the corner near the (London-Southampton) **railway** (550m).
⑦ Cross the end of the pond next to the station car park (350m).
⑧ Bear R on the side path round the corner of the pond (50m) then diverge L up the bank. Keep to paths near the top of the bank until the only onward path drops off the bank R (650m). Just before the drop, turn L out of the trees (20m).
ⓔ *Extension of 1 km/¾ mile: Go round the L edge of the fields and back along the top edge (1000m).*
ⓕ *At the hedge cut L through the trees (30m). Continue on the track (R) down to the bridge (500m).* ➔⑩
⑨ Go up the edge of the field R to the vehicle track (250m). Follow the the track R to the bridge at the track/path junction (300m).
⑩ Stay on the main track, now diverging from the stream (300m).
⑪ On the R bend watch out for a side path L and ascend, forking R, to the fence of **Pystock** Research Station (150m). Follow the fence R and find a path down R, just after the two circular tanks (250m).
⑫ Descend back to the main track (80m). Start along the side track opposite (30m) and fork L Disregard the side track diverging R and climb to the top (300m). ★
⑬ When the track bends downhill R, take branch paths L to the road (100m). Go R along the pavement over the canal (100m).
⑭ Cross the main road and go up the heath path to the track junction on top (100m). Disregard the track ahead and the track L and bear L on the track between them down the slope and round a R curve (200m). Stay on this track, over the culverted Gelvert Stream (300m). and up to the car park (350m).
The uphill track behind the car park leads to the ***Foresters*** (100m). ✾

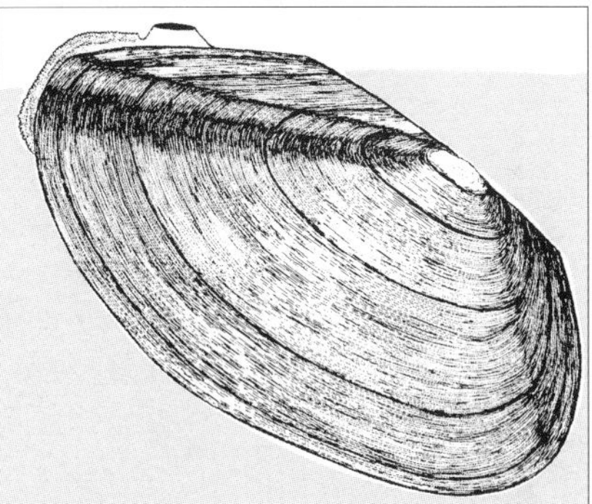

Swan Mussels, up to 10cm/4" long, live in the mud on the bottom of Fleet Pond and used to be eaten. They draw in a current of water from which they filter planktonic food. The larvae travel and feed embedded in the skin of sticklebacks as parasites .

The Lamellibranchiata (bivalves or two-shelled molluscs) are generally perceived as sea animals but there are many freshwater species.

41 Beacon Hill, Ewshot and Tweseldown

About 9 km/5½ miles with two extensions of 1½ km/1 mile to Cæsar's Camp and the *Foresters Inn*. Mainly heath; short very steep slopes. On race days avoid Tweseldown. OS maps 1:25000 145 Guildford, 1:50000 186 Aldershot.

Start from a Bourley Road car park, SU 831 510, in a dip near Bourley Lane or from the recreation ground car park at Ewshot, SU 816 502.

The Windmill ☎ 01250 850439 ***The Foresters*** ☎ 01252 616503

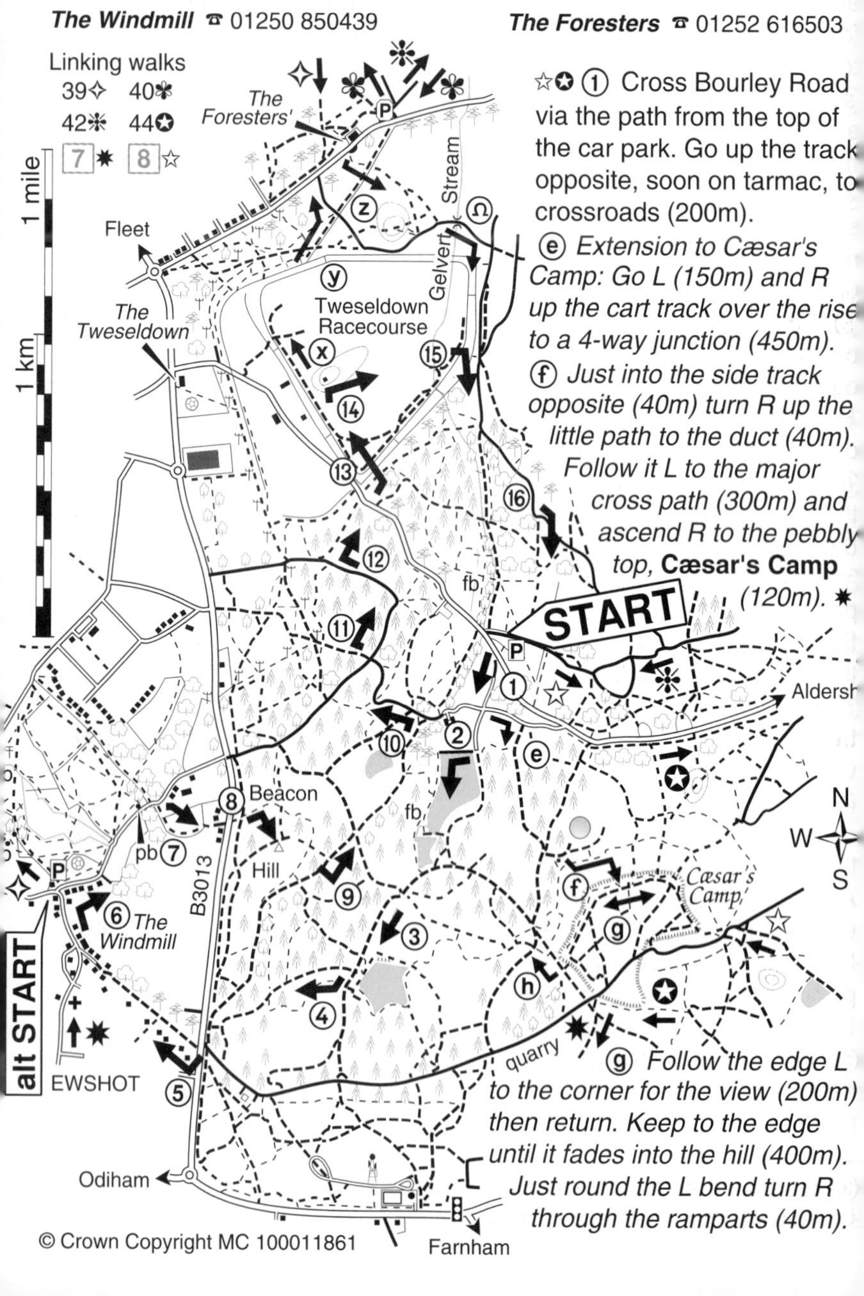

☆✪ ① Cross Bourley Road via the path from the top of the car park. Go up the track opposite, soon on tarmac, to crossroads (200m).

ⓔ *Extension to Cæsar's Camp: Go L (150m) and R up the cart track over the rise to a 4-way junction (450m).*

ⓕ *Just into the side track opposite (40m) turn R up the little path to the duct (40m). Follow it L to the major cross path (300m) and ascend R to the pebbly top,* **Cæsar's Camp** *(120m).* ✸

ⓖ *Follow the edge L to the corner for the view (200m) then return. Keep to the edge until it fades into the hill (400m). Just round the L bend turn R through the ramparts (40m).*

ⓗ Turn R immediately down the hill (200m) and fork L, passing reservoirs R (500m). ➔③

② Keep on up to the reservoir (**Army Waterworks**)(150m) then then turn R and skirt round the edge (350m). Just before the footbridge fork R past the top pond to the track (200m). Go R (80m).

③ At the 5-way junction continue ahead up round the bend to the next pond L (200m).

④ Disregard the track R at the start of the pond, but turn onto the next side track R (50m). Stay on it up to the T-junction (150m).

⑤ Go R to the road (100m) and cross to the track slightly L on the other side. Follow it down to the *Windmill* in **Ewshot** (550m). Keep on to the road junction (200m). ✧

⑥ Go R on Tadpole Lane or along the fields beside it to the **pillbox** at the bend under trees (500m).

⑦ Just after the S-bend take the path R up round the edge of the fields (250m). At the house go R to the road - nasty crossing (100m).

⑧ Slightly R (10m) go through the trees opposite to the track (70m). Cross it and follow the water duct (150m). After the R curve cross the culvert and climb the steep path to the flat top of **Beacon Hill** (100m). A track comes past the trig point to end on the corner of the **plateau**. Drop off this corner down the steep path, over a runnel, to the hard track (150m).

⑨ Walk down the track L, over a 4-way junction (100m), past the pond L (250m) and round L & R curves to a T-junction (200m).

⑩ Go L on the track up round a U-bend to the cross track (250m).

⑪ Turn R. The track drops then rises through forestry plantations and bends on the top (250m). Continue down into a dip (200m) and up the other side (100m).

⑫ Just over the brow, take the 1st path R down to the road (250m). Cross into the trees and go L to **Tweseldown** Racecourse (30m).

⑬ Cross the race track and make for the tower on the hilltop (400m).

ⓧ Extension to The Foresters: Go on beside the race track (300m) and round the top bend (150m).

ⓨ After the high point (100m) take the diverging path from the outer edge, to a path junction (50m) and ahead to the cart track (150m). Go L to the road (100m) and R on the track on the other side (100m). ✻✻

*ⓩ From the parking area opposite the **Foresters** drop to the heath. Follow the path away from the road skirting L of the hillock to join the hard track after it (400m).*

Ⓘ Go L to the junction outside the bottom of the race track (250m) then R parallel with the course until it bends away (300m). ➔⑮

⑭ Turn R towards **Farnborough Airport**. Identify the bottom R bend in the race track and make for it (400m). From the stream and water jumps cross the race track obliquely to the edge just before the end of the curve (150m) and find the path out to the track junction (40m). Turn R.

⑮ Take the R-most track to the next junction (200m) and bear L on the main track over a hillock and round curves (350m).

⑯ At the S-bend take the side track ahead to the end (200m) and bear R to the car park (200m).

42 Claycart, Long Valley and Basingstoke Canal

About 8½ km/5¼ miles with extensions of 1 km/¾ mile and ½ km/⅓ mile: canal towpath and heath, undulating: mainly army land where you may pass through a miltary exercise. OS maps 1:25000 145 Guildford, 1:50000 186 Aldershot.

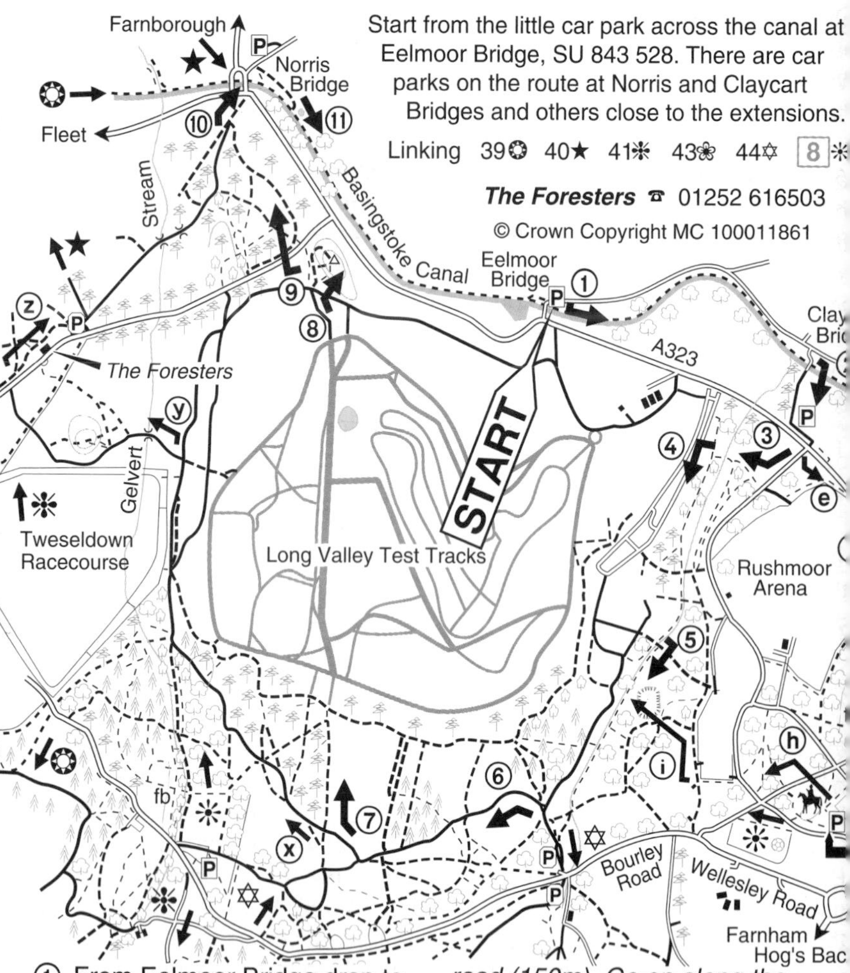

Start from the little car park across the canal at Eelmoor Bridge, SU 843 528. There are car parks on the route at Norris and Claycart Bridges and others close to the extensions.

Linking 39✪ 40★ 41✻ 43❀ 44✡ 8 ✻

The Foresters ☎ 01252 616503

① From Eelmoor Bridge drop to the **Basingstoke Canal** and walk L along the towpath (1200m). ❀

② Cross Claycart Bridge and aim L over the grass for the exit of the car park at the top (250m).

ⓔ *Extension of 1 km/¾ mile to* **Bat's Hogsty***: Go up the side road opposite the car park a little then cross through the wood L to the fence and follow it down to the road (150m). Go on along the pavement to the bend (200m).*

ⓕ *Bear R along the track by the fence (100m). When it curves R, go L into the wood, over a culvert and up to the sports field (200m). Cross the R corner to the end of the trees (200m).*

ⓖ *Continue on the track between fields (300m). Cross the little road and go on along the fields on the ath or on the grass or through the plendid wood (300m). After the ext road cross the sunken field to e furthest corner (200m).* ✳

) *From the Garrison Church car ark go over the knoll R of the* **Vellington Statue** *and down to e road behind (150m). Opposite gateway go on through the wood 50m) then steer L at a right angle no path)(150m). If you hit the road t the wrong point, look for a fence orner on the other side at the end. Follow the path away from e road beside the fence (80m).*

) *Turn R down the track beside e fence (150m) then L down the curving side track (150m). Just round the L bend, fork R briefly then cross the fence R into Bat's Hogsty (no paths). Make your way to the bottom L (100m) then more steeply to the Claycart Stream (50m). Turn L.* ➜⑤

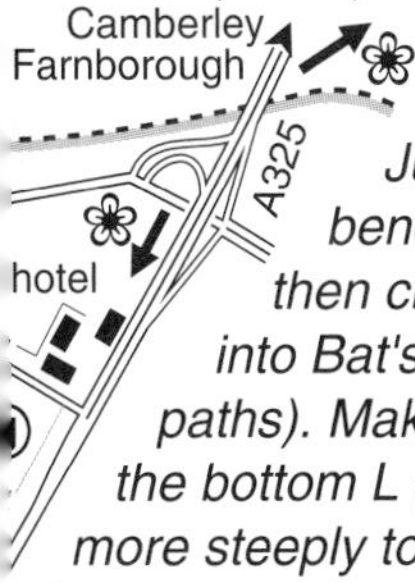

Camberley
Farnborough
A325
hotel

) Go up the side road, opposite e car park, and diverge slightly R rough the trees (no path)(200m). urn R down the small path from e road (opposite a track) (100m) nd R at the bottom (80m).

) At the rise turn L. Go along the hady path at the foot of the bank r along the grass on top (300m). urve L with the path to a cross ack (150m). Go on along Claycart tream to the cross track after the curve (300m). Cross the stream nd continue on the other side.

) Stay beside the stream to the ext track (650m) then go R 100m) (or ahead if making for the rossways parking area ✡).

⑥ At the junction take the main uphill track curving L. Continue over the top, ahead at the cross-track (650m), ✳ down round the R bend in the defile (100m) and over to the next cross track (150m).

ⓧ *Extension of ½ km/1/3 mile to the* ***Foresters****: Stay ahead on the undulating, winding main track to* **Tweseldown** *Racecourse, visible L through the trees (1400m).* ✪

ⓨ *Turn L at the side track after the racecourse, up to the road (700m).*

ⓩ *On the other side follow the track R to the pub (150m).* ★ *Pass behind the pub down to the heath car park (100m). Take the downhill track (650m) and stay on it winding to the flat top of a hill (200m).* ➜⑩

⑦ Go down the side track R to the bottom (400m). Stay ahead to the Long Valley test track complex and along the very wide track (1200m). Fork L when it splits near the end, (150m). Cross a wide track and follow the smaller track (150m).

⑧ Over the next cross track go straight up the knoll R, overlooking **Farnborough Airport** (150m).

⑨ Drop back off the knoll via the track opposite the trig point (70m) and turn ½R on the little path to the fast road (100m). Cross and go R on the rising track (500m).

⑩ From the 4-way junction drop to the main road at Norris Bridge (150m). Cross the canal via the R side of the R bridge to the 1st side road R and the track R (50m).

⑪ At the track drop to the canal R via the break-neck path (30m) or continue ahead converging on the canal (200m). Carry on (L) along the towpath past the end of the runway to Eelmoor Bridge (1300m).

43 Around North Camp

About 7½ km/4¾ miles, along the Basingstoke Canal and the Blackwater River and through the military town; level; suitable for wheel chairs. The extension of ¾ km/½ mile uses more canal but has a long road section. OS maps 1:25000 145 Guildford, 1:50000 186 Aldershot.

Linking walks 42❀ 35✸ 36❊

Start from the army car park on Queen's Avenue, Aldershot (near the canal), SU 867 522, or North Camp car park, SU 873 534, or the service road near North Camp Station, SU 880 537, or Lakeside Road car park, SU 889 518.

The Old Ford ☎ 01252 544840 ***The Standard of England*** ☎ 01252 325539
The Swan ☎ 01252 325212 **Aldershot Military Museum** ☎ 01252 314598

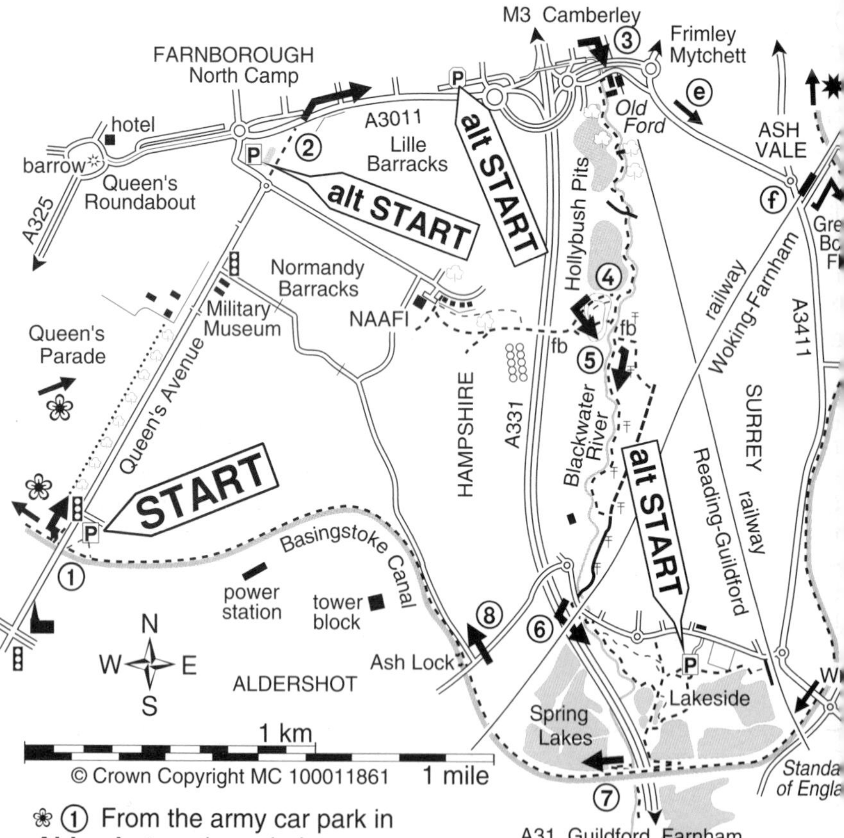

❀ ① From the army car park in **Aldershot** go through the trees to the canal (50m) Pass under the iron bridge then up R to open fields (**Queen's Parade**). Carry straight on over the grass or under the trees parallel with Queen's Avenue (opposite Army Physical Training School) to the end of the sports field (900m).Go on along the grass or the pavement, past the **Military Museum**, opposite (500m). When the road bends L stay ahead past the pond (200m).

) Cross the main road to the ɜrvice road. Turn R and follow the ·ad past all the shops and down '00m). Cross the long footbridge ver the A331 (150m). Stay on the ɜrvice road to the end (50m) then ıss under the main road to nerge near **North Camp** Station nd the ***Old Ford*** pub (100m). ❊

) *Extension of ¾ km/½ mile: ross the railway and go on along e main road to Ash Vale (800m).*

) *Walk under the railway bridge nd L up past the station to the ɜnal (200m). Follow the towpath ' to the aqueduct (2600m).* ➧⑦

) Find the footbridge over the ackwater **River** and follow the inding footpath beside it (900m).

) After the last of the Hollybush it lakes, fork R up the small hill 00m). Pass over the top then L ɜck to the original path (50m).

⑤ Cross the footbridge and keep on beside the winding river until the path joins a wider track (750m) then go R to the road (300m).

⑥ Don't go along the road. Cross to the path behind the emergency pumping station. Pass under the **railway** (Woking to Farnham) and over the river (100m). Carry on to join another path (300m). Go R between gravel pits (300m), up the ramp to the **Basingstoke Canal** (100m) and onto the aqueduct above the A331 (100m).

⑦ Keep on along the canal on the embankment under the railway bridge (600m) to the road (200m).

⑧ Go under or over the road to Ash Lock and on along the tow-path past the army power station (with six chimneys) to the next road (1800m). Side paths just before it lead to the car park.

The view from the Basingstoke Canal aqueduct:
Beneath, are the A331 and the infant Blackwater River much re-channelled for the building of the road. The length of the canal embankment shows how broad the Blackwater valley is compared with the trickle of the present river. Southwards the Hog's Back is visible over Ash Church. The tower block to the NW is the military catering school in Aldershot. Below, the mound is an artificial bat cave constructed as part of the road building plan. Extraction of gravel (Terraces 1 & 2 Devensian) during the 20th century left the flooded pits. They have a low pH, contrasting with the Basingstoke Canal which receives most of its water from springs in the chalk tunnel at Greywell with a high pH. Thus there is a rich aquatic flora in the area.

The A331, Blackwater Valley Relief Road, passing under the aqueduct was completed in 1996. It follows the marshy valley, crossing the old Hampshire/ Surrey border repeatedly. Troughs sunk in the London Clay 15m below the water table take the road under the canal and railway. They are weighted with extra concrete to stop them floating up. The 60cm thick plates are set in a dihedral under the road with neoprene hinges at the middle and edges so that, if the road sinks, the centre is raised, forcing the sides out to lock the structure in the ground. The troughs have emergency pumps. The county boundary is now along the midle of the road

44 Blackwater Source and Cæsar's Camp

About 7 km/4¼ miles; heath and wood with confusing, stony tracks and very steep short sections; extending 2 km/1¼ miles to the Wellington Statue. As we as getting lost, you may find yourself in an army exercise with rifle shooting (blanks). OS maps 1:25000 145 Guildford, 1:50000 186 Aldershot.

Start at Rowhill car park, Cranmore Lane, Aldershot, SU 848 500, or Crossway car parks, Bourley Road, SU 844 509. On the extension, start from the car par at the Welllington Statue, SU 853 511.

Linking 41✪ 42✡ 7✷ 8✦

The Royal Arms 01252 320149

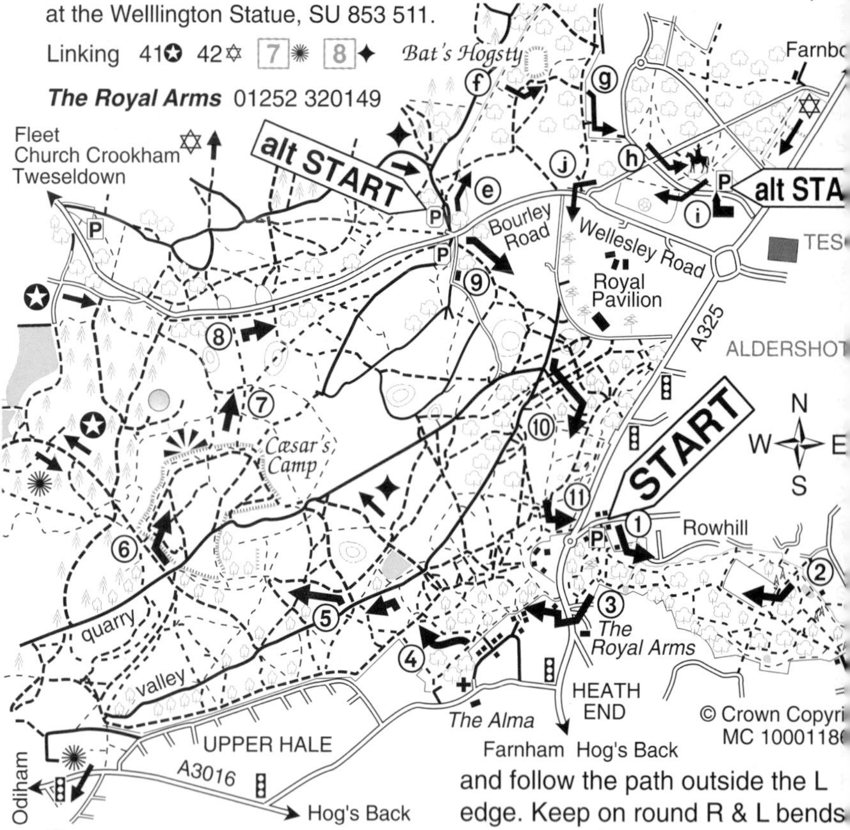

① At Rowhill car park, **Aldershot**, follow the track next to the house away from the road (100m). Just after the last garden (10m) turn L down the little path (100m). Cross a brook, the infant Blackwater **River**, and go on (100m). At the R bend turn down the side path L and continue beside the brook to the tarmac path from the road (500m).

② Go R up the path until level with the field (100m) then cut the corner and follow the path outside the L edge. Keep on round R & L bends to the pond (550m) and up to the source of the Blackwater (150m).

③ From the bend, zig-zag up the steps (30m) and turn L to the road (150m). The ***Royal Arms*** is 80m L Crossing is hazardous. Look over the main road for the path at the R end of the garden wall. Cross to the L then go along the wall (40m) Climb the steep path and continue along the garden fences to a wide track L between gardens (350m).

④ Turn R up through the trees and stay ahead to the ridge track (300m). Cross the track and, slightly L, go down the steep path, to the pond (80m). ✦ Walk up the valley track L to the track junction after the pond (120). ✷

⑤ Turn R on the side track (80m) and L up the cross track. When the track shrinks (300m) keep to the path ahead past **Cæsar's Camp** R (200m) and outside the ramparts up to the next hard track (150m). Continue on the other side, 20m L, still outside ramparts (150m). ✪

⑥ At the edge of the **plateau** turn R through the ramparts and follow the little path along the edge (300m). Go round a bend in the edge of the plateau overlooking the **Army Waterworks** covered reservoir and on to the next bend (300m) overlooking the N Downs.

⑦ Go back (50m) then down the very steep path through the pebble layer, over the water duct (100m) to the track junction (100m). Stay ahead down between knolls almost to Bourley Road (250m). ✡

⑧ Turn R on the path near the road and keep to it all the way down to the Crossways parking area - tracks with parking spaces on both sides of the road (850m).

ⓔ *Extension of 2 km/1¼ miles to the* **Wellington Statue***: Walk up through the parking area on the N side of the road (120m) and bear R on the next side track (120m). After the cross track follow the little path beside the Claycart Stream. Watch out for a little water chute then a pipe crossing the stream (300m).*

ⓕ *After the pipe (15m) take the little path R up to the track (100m). Go L on the track round a R bend (near* **Bat's Hogsty***) (100m) and up to the boundary track (200m).*

ⓖ *Go R on the track to the orner of the fence (200m) then L on the path beside the fence (150m).*

ⓗ *Walk R along the road (100m), over the crossroads (100m) then L up the knoll to the statue and down towards the church (100m).*

ⓘ *From the car park walk go over the grass L of the knoll with the statue (100m) then cross the road and go through the football field to the gateway at the far end (200m). Go L up the road (200m) and R on the verge of Bourley Road (80m).*

ⓙ *Cross to the concrete track and follow it up the boundary (300m). When it curves L at the top, fork R on the hard track up over the little ridge (200m).* ➜⑩

⑨ From the parking area on the S side of the road cross the ditch (Claycart Stream) to the adjacent army road. Just into it (20m) turn L up the side track. Avoid R forks and keep on to the major hard track on top (450m) then turn R over the little ridge (100m).

⑩ Go on down to the junction with the hard track R (100m) then bear L over the open space. Cross several tracks and rise steeply to the ridge - traffic is usually audible (200m). Walk up the ridge path R and through a complex of tracks at a concrete wall (400m).

⑪ Bear L on the straight sunken path down the flank of the ridge (50m) then drop L beside the fence to the road (100m). Cross the main road and go down the side road to the car park beside the first house R (100m).

Aldershot became the home of the British Army when the Government bought large tracts of heath in 1854. It was part of Domesday Book Crondall but is first heard of as the hamlet, *Alreshute*, in a list of 1316. The medieval church, St Michael, probably derives from a chapel of Crondall which existed before 1400.

Ambarrow Court was a large house. It has been demolished and the grounds, with hill, belong to the National Trust. During World War II it was a secret RADAR countermeasures research station of the Royal Aircraft Establishment.

The **Arboretum** at Windlesham is a charitable trust and allows free access to pedestrians during the hours of daylight; parts are open only by invitation. Planting started in 1960 but there are mature trees of a former nursery. Near the brook, excavation yielded Saxon, Roman and Iron Age finds, including a coin of Addedomarus, of about 20 BC, King of the Trinovantes (an Essex tribe).

Arborfield was not a Domesday Book manor, but was probably detached in the 13th century from the Sonning estate of the Bishops of Salisbury which would account for Arborfield being an enclave of Wiltshire until the 19th century. The modern manor house became part of the National Institute for Research in Dairying and is featured anonymously in *Our Village* by Mary Russel Mitford. The Church, St Bartholomew's, is an airy Victorian building (1863) which replaced the earlier crumbling church. Points of interest: the flint façade; the reclining alabaster figure of William Standon, d 1639, who claimed to be an Atrebate; the memorial tablet above Wm Standon which cuttingly declines to comment. The Arborfield Army Camp is mainly in Barkham Parish. It started as an army remount depot before the Great War, collecting and distributing large numbers of horses. It is now the home of REME and their main training centre for radio and radar technicians. It has a public museum.

The **Army Power Station**, when built in 1961, gave the military town an independent electricity supply. It supplies hot water to heat army buildings and now sells electricity to the national grid.

The **Army waterworks**, constructed around 1865, are still in use as the water is cheaper than the public supply. Ceramic and brick runnels around Cæsar's Camp and Beacon Hill catch run off and take the water to the open ponds. After the treatment plant, it is pumped up to the circular covered reservoir.

Ash Lock (29) is at approximately the mid point on the Basingstoke Canal but is the highest lock, the canal being level to Basingstoke.

Bagshot records are bedevilled by conflicting uses of the name. Bagshot was the Surrey bailiwick of Windsor Forest as well as the Royal Park, manor, village and parish. It was *Bagshete* in the pipe roll of 1164, possibly from Bacga's sceat; *Bacga*, a Saxon personal name; *sceat*, a corner of land. It was not a manor in the Domesday Book but there are records of a small estate of agricultural land in the medieval period. Inns are prominent in the records and it is likely the village developed because of the great west road to Winchester, Southampton, Salisbury and Exeter. A John Hostiller of Bagshote was plaintiff in a theft case in 1417 but the earliest recorded by name was *The Crown,* in a rental of 1515. The church, St Anne's, was built in 1884, Bagshot being part of Windlesham Parish until 1874. A guild was licensed in 1480 to fund St Mary's chapel (of Windlesham) at Bagshot as a cooperative chantry.

A History of Bagshot and Windlesham Marie Eddle 1977 Phillimore 262pp

Bagshot Heath of old was a large wild area in the corners of Berkshire, Surrey and Hampshire between Bagshot and Hartley Wintney crossed by the arterial west road to Exeter (now the A30). Defoe wrote in 1722: *I took the Winchester Coach ... dined at a small village called Egham and from thence through the* *orst heathy country I ever saw ... 18 miles to Farnham*; William Cobbett in 322 described a spot in the New Forest as *more barren and miserable than agshot Heath*. Much of the heath has disappeared under Camberley, Fleet, arnborough and Yateley and forestry plantations. The large remnant between amberley and Bracknell is the 19th century commons of Windlesham and rimley and Crown Land which was heath in the Swinley Bailiwick of Windsor orest. There was a World War II German prisoner-of war-camp on Old Dean ommon where the housing estate is now; the prisoners worked in Camberley.

agshot Park is a royal estate of 320 acres with 81 acres of parkland. From e middle ages it was the site of a royal hunting lodge. The earliest reference the park was the grant of office of keeper to William Mitchell in 1486. The tuart kings made frequent use of the lodge but, after Charles II, its resident ingers were royal relatives or high officials. On a different site, the present udoresque house in red brick and Portland stone is the principal residence of RH The Earl of Wessex. It was built in 1857 for the 3rd son of Queen Victoria, e Duke of Connaught (1850-1942). A professional soldier, he rose from cadet Sandhurst to C-in-C, Aldershot in the 1890s and was Governor General of anada 1911-16. It was HQ of the Army Chaplains' Department 1946-96.

arkham first appears in writing as BEORCHAM in 952 in a grant by Eadred, ng of Wessex. The present Manor House, now flats, was built around 1700 ut has Georgian and Victorian additions. The ornamental pond was the stew r storing live fish and may have been a moat. George Washington's mother, ary Ball, came from a Barkham family. There is a record of sale for The Bull ehouse in 1749. Barkham's last Court Baron (manorial land board) was held ere in 1846. The Church, St James the Apostle, consecrated 1861, was built y John Walter III of Bearwood who bought Barkham Manor in 1874 - the latest a long line of churches on this spot since Norman times. No church is listed the Domesday Book and the earliest record is for the advowson in 1220. he anonymous wooden figure may be Agnes de Nevile whose ownership of e manor was disputed in the 1330s. David Davis, rector 1782-1819, figures in ocial history. He grew up in Barbados and gave evidence against slavery; as hampion of farm workers, he wrote the treatise *The Case for Labourers in usbandry Stated and Considered*. The moat near the church was probably for e medieval manor house. *Barkham, 952-1990* Richard Noble 1994 38pp

arkham Brook drains westward to the River Loddon.

arossa Common is part of **Bagshot Heath** which has had its commoners' ghts extinguished to form an army training area. The Surrey part was common nd of Frimley and the Berkshire part was Windsor Forest. The fenced part as rifle ranges for the military academy.

he **Basingstoke Canal** is 37 miles long. It starts at Byfleet where it joined the ey Navigation in 1796 at the apogee of the British canal building period. It did ot pay for itself. Agricultural produce was conveyed to London; coal and orse dung brought back. The last large contract was to carry bricks from Up ateley for re-building Aldershot army camp at the end of the 19th century. No arges reached Basingstoke after 1910. It is now owned jointly by Surrey and ants County Councils. Cut by the M3, it is navigable only as far as Odiham astle. *London's Lost Route to Basingstoke* P A L Vine 1968 David & Charles 212pp

at's Hogsty is a curiosity amongst walkers because of its name and because ey cannot find it; amongst archæologists because they cannot decide what it as for. It is a rectangle of about ¾ acre enclosed by four mounds with three itches between them, externally 300' x 270', in total about 1¾ acres.
The Bat's Hogsty Earthworks D Westlake Aldershot Hist & Arch Soc 1983 & 84

Beacon Hill is on similar terrain to Cæsar's Camp. The trig point was built in 1951 at a cost of £11 10s 9d. Two beacons are shown on the hill in Norden's map of 1595. This Crondall beacon site was part of a county network fanning out from the Isle of Wight. Beacons told of the fall of Troy in 1084 BC but the first record of English beacons appears in 1324 when Edward II made ready for invasion by his queen. From Dogmersfield in 1468 Edward IV ordered the beacons to be maintained. A French report in 1539 suggests the deterrent value of the beacons. Walsingham obtained an analysis of the forces mustered when the beacons were lit for the Armada in 1588. The last-known record is for a trial of beacons in Devon in 1638. Early beacons were piles of timber. Later, a barrel of pitch was specified and payments for constructing beacons and keeping watch were made from parish funds. Symbols on an old map show beacons as of iron baskets on poles but these may have been small ones for short distances. The word comes from the Saxon *beacnian*, to beckon, but place-names like Beaconsfield sometimes derive from the Saxon man's name *Beca*.

The Beacon System in Hampshire H T White Proc Hants Field Club Vol X 1931 28pp

Blackbushe Airfield is a civil aviation complex for small aircraft. It was built in 1941-42 on requisitioned land called Hartford Bridge Flats. Before the runways were ready the Royal Aircraft Establishment held glider trials. It was home to a succession of squadrons flying Mustangs, Tomahawks, Blenheims, Lockhead Venturas, Mosquitos, Mitchell bombers and Spitfires. The Free French Lorrain Squadron carried out daylight bombing on V-I sites. Mitchell bombers went to the bridge too far, Arnhem. Spitfires shot up the Calais area as a feint prior to D-Day in Operation Starkey. General Eisenhower visited in April 1944. King George VI visited in July 1944. Latterly it was Transport Command's base and the forerunner of civilian services to the Channel Islands. Aircraft used to be towed to hangers across the A30. The airfield stands on a plateau (Terrace 7).

Hampshire Airfields in the Second World War R Brooks 1996 Countryside Books 192pp

Borough Court is an ancient house. The core of the building is a 5-bay timber framed hall of about 1480. John Fielder bought it in 1561 which is when the high chimneys were added. Only four families have owned it.

Bramshill is said to be the finest Jacobean house in Hampshire. It was the Red Cross HQ for World War II and residence of the King of Romania in exile. The Home Office purchased the estate in 1953 and made the house into the Police Staff College for England and Wales, BROMSELLE was the name of two Domesday Book manors belonging to the Norman Baron Hugh de Port of Basing. The estate had many occupiers and was emparked around 1350. Edward Zouche, 1556?-1625, 11th Baron Harringworth built the present house using the foundations and walls of earlier houses. He was a minor government official under Elizabeth I but became more prominent under James I; the long building period, 1605-1625, and mean plan suggest he was not over-wealthy. A keen horticulturalist, he is sometimes credited with or blamed for introducing the Scots Pine to the south of England. Jonson's masque *Lovers Made Men* was written for Bramshill in 1617 - said to be the first operatic performance in English. It was during a visit to consecrate the Bramshill chapel that George Abbott, Archbishop of Canterbury (his tomb is in Holy Trinity, Guildford), went hunting and accidentally shot the gamekeeper. Peter Hawkins lost his life; the Archbishop lost face.

Bramshill House official guide Helen Hills 22pp

Bramshill Forest is a modern name for the Forestry Commission plantations on the Bramshill estate and elsewhere, nearby. The slope into Bramshill Park is the western edge of the Yateley Heath gravel capped plateau (Terrace 7, Anglian Glaciation, 47-59 000 years BP). Sand and gravel workings have scarred the lower parts and some of the pits have been filled with refuse.

roadmoor Hospital is one of three institutions for the dangerously insane. In)05 there were 273 patients (42 women) and about 1500 staff. Most patients rive as a result of criminal trials but a few are from other psychiatric hospitals. 1800 James Hadfield tried to shoot George III but was denied his wish to be ıng, drawn and quartered for treason being found to be mad. This precedent timately led to an Act of 1860 establishing the Broadmoor Criminal Lunatic sylum. The secure part was 10 acres for men and 3½ for women and 150 cres of farmland were appended. The main buildings in "Prison Romanesque" ere by Sir Joshua Jebb. Broadmoor remained under the Home Office until 948 thereafter being the province of the Ministry of Health. Since 1960 it has een called Broadmoor Hospital. Useful alumni have been Richard Dadd the ainter (42 years) and Dr Minors, the Oxford Dictionary scholar (around 1900).

æsar's Camp, near Bracknell, is an Iron Age fort of about 700 BC, on a atural promontory of the plateau, fortified on the flanks by two banks and a tch (with logs to deter motorcyclists). The level southern end has an extra ank and ditch. Between here and the Devil's Highway at Wickham Bushes, oman pots and a brick floor have been found, possibly a military staging post.

æsar's Camp, near Farnham, is an Iron Age promontory fort of 28 acres on ateau gravel of a pre-Anglian glaciation, 60m/200 feet above the present-day ource of the Blackwater River. The flat parts have double and treble ramparts ut the scarp is very steep and was probably never needed fortification. The raight mound across the middle is the county boundary and has post holes of e 12th century pale of the Bishop of Winchester's Farnham deer park. ebbles of the plateau cap were quarried outside the ramparts and are seen in ictorian buildings of the area. The splendid view is across the vast valley of e Blackwater River and along the London Basin. In fine weather the tall uildings of London may be seen. The Battle of Farnham, reported in the nglo-Saxon Chronicle for 893, is said to have taken place below Cæsar's amp. Alfred the Great had already made peace with settler Vikings but a iding group came to Kent after several years in France. He brought them to attle here, won and recaptured booty, then chased them over the Thames.

alifornia Country Park was a holiday camp in the 1920s & 30s with ballroom, oo, speedway and steam railway, said to be the inspiration for the Pontin amps. Longmoor Pond started as a claypit in the 1850s. Some of the bricks ere used to build Bearwood. The boggy heath NW of the pond is a SSSI.

amberley had a curious origin as a 19th Century spontaneous new town with o previous settlement on the heath of Frimley Manor. The impetus was the oyal Military College Sandhurst for which construction workers' houses were uilt in 1802. The Duke of York Hotel, built for visitors, became a nucleus for ther service providers. When the Staff College opened in 1862 the Duke of ambridge Hotel accommodated its visitors and became another nucleus - ence Yorktown and Cambridgetown. The GPO devised the name Camberley 1877 to avoid confusion with Cambridge. Much of the land sold from Frimley lanor became extensive grounds for large houses and the modern housing states have arisen by the redevelopment of these, which infill continues.

The Story of Camberley 1798-1987 Gordon Wellard 1989 134pp

EDAR is the Centre for Dairy Research, part of the Department of Agriculture f Reading University but one of the world's leading research centres on ovine health largely funding itself from research contracts and a levy on milk roducers. The farm has 645 hectares of grazing and forage land and 450 attle. On the same site are the Animal Production Unit, The Veterinary pidemiology and Economic Research Unit.

Chequers Bridge takes its name from the nearby pub which accommodated workers and horses during the building of the canal. The car park occupies the Crondall wharf. The house nearest the bridge is thought to have been the original office of the canal company. From here to Blacksmith's Bridge are several WWII pillboxes and large concrete blocks for obstructing the canal.

Crondall was the Domesday Book Hundred of CORENDEL with the manors of Crondall (CRVNDELE), Cove, Itchel, Farnborough, Long Sutton and Badley. It appears in Alfred the Great's will, drafted *circa* 885, as a bequest to Ethelm, his nephew. *He* passed it to St Swithun's Abbey, Winchester. After the Dissolution in 1539, it was granted to the Dean & Chapter. The roads reflect the Saxon layout; there are houses of all periods from 1475. The *Plume of Feathers* on its prime site was probably always an inn. The jettied part dates from about 1500; the middle part would have replaced an earlier hall house a bit later. The front parlour has a dragon beam to support the joists for jettying on two sides and the corner. It is said Cromwell stayed in October 1645, on the way to the siege of Basing House. The church, All Saints, was built when styles were changing in the 12th century with Norman round arches in the nave but slightly pointed arches in the chancel. The clerestory arches are Victorian brick restorations. Features of interest: the east end of the aisles distorted by the original central tower (replaced by the brick north tower in 1657 for £428), the slanting chancel arch pillars, the possible Saxon font, a large brass of about 1380 in the chancel floor. *Medieval Houses in Crondall* M A Jeffries *Crondall Society News*

Crookham was part of the great Domesday Book estate of Crondall, belonging to the monastery in Winchester from the Saxon era. The name first appears in writing in 1257 when the Prior and Convent of St Swithun granted to *Henry called the hunter our bailiff ... land ... in Crokeham formerly held of us in villeinage* - for 30 marks down + 60 shillings pa. It was a hamlet and tithing of Crondall until the parish was detached in 1842 with the new Christ Church. Crookham and Fleet became civil parishes in 1894 with the canal as boundary.

Crowthorne developed on empty heath, at the building of Wellington College and Broadmoor in the 19th century. The name first appears in Norden's map of 1607 where it seems to label a tree, perhaps a boundary mark, at the juncture of three forest walks (Bigshot, Sandhurst and Easthampstead) and four tracks. The area was part of the Windsor Forest and the only ancient records are the proceedings of the swainmote (Forest court) at Wokingham which go back to 1586. The forest was broken up in 1800 when allotments were made to local landholders. Most of the village lay in the ancient parish of Sandhurst. The Church, St John the Baptist, was consecrated in 1873 and Crowthorne became a parish in 1874. The Road Research Laboratory was hived off from the National Physical Laboratory Teddington in 1953 but is an independent company now, TRL. It does research on all aspects of land transport, statistical as well as vehicle testing and road construction. It occupies 253 acres.

The Crow on the Thorn Martin Prescott 1975 347pp

Curzon Bridges are on the line of the pre-railway road from Frimley to Guildford. The wall below on the east side was required under the railway Act to prevent canal horses being frightened by steam engines.

Deepcut village takes its name from the canal which was cut through the hills in the late 1780s before the era of power tools and vehicles. Most of the sand removed went to build the embankment across the Blackwater Valley. Deepcut army depot is now the home of the Royal Logistics Corps. The track through the wood on the north side of the canal runs on the line of the army railway, the WWI extension of the Bisley line which crossed the canal near lock 15.

evil's Highway Roman road - see box on page 15.

ipley Mill is a picturesque dwelling best seen from the road bridge over the 'hitewater River. It may be on the site of the Mattingley mill recorded in the omesday Book The last miller was William White who worked it from 1905. It ad two undershot wheels and was converted to a house in 1921. The garden ied is a pillbox and there are World War II blocks at the road bridge.

ogmersfield was the Domesday Book manor of ORMERESFELT which was xed for 100 pigs @100 shillings. It was given to the Bishop of Durham in the ne of Henry I. From the 12th century until bought by Henry VIII it belonged to e Bishops of Bath & Wells, who lived there. The mediaeval church was near e house but was pulled down in 1806. The present village is a fusion of Pilcot nd Chatter Alley hamlets with a Victorian church, All Saints. Pilcot had a mill.

ogmersfield Park is a Queen Anne mansion built in 1728 but much restored fter a serious fire in 1982. It is now a hotel but has been a college of the de alle Brothers and HQ of the US computing company Amdahl. Henry VII rode ith his son, Arthur, to the Tudor bishop's palace here to greet Catherine of ragon on her arrival in England, hence the *Queen's Head* in the village.

versley was part of Edward the Confessor's endowment of Westminster bbey. A translation of the charter of about 1060 is displayed in the church. he Domesday Book indicates it had been four manors with two mills. After the onquest it remained Abbey property. In the 15th century its dues consisted of sparrow hawk. The church, St Mary, is not mentioned in the Domesday Book ut a valuation of the benefice (£8) exists from 1235 and a sarsen under the ap door near the font suggests a pre-Christian site of worship. The chancel ates from about 1500 and the nave from 1735. Charles Kingsley was rector 844-1875. Points of interest: the barrel vaulting of the roof (1876); the chancel creen (1730), the only 18th century one in Hampshire; the brass memorial 'oss of 1502 in the chancel floor; the south window of the chancel, 1942, with vo water babies and fishing rod; Charles Kingsley's grave near the wall on the 'ectory side; the Wellingtonia potted as a seed in 1875 by his daughter.

wshot was hived off as a parish from Crondall and Crookham in 1886. It first ppears in records of 1279 as land of the Bishop of Worcester - a Giffard. The nurch, St Mary's, suits this period but is Victorian (built 1873).

arnborough Airport is now largely civil being used by air taxis and private wners. It was the Royal Aircraft Establishment, 1918-1991, which originated s an army balloon factory built in 1905. By WWI it was the Royal Aircraft actory but changed to RAE when the RAF was created in 1918. It went on to e world leader in aluminium alloys, carbon fibre, radio, aviation medicine and rash investigation and still has a defence research presence. The airfield was fighter base in WWII. The Farnborough Air Sciences Trust Museum is chiefly bout research and development and occupies the Balloon School building. arnborough itself straddles the Portsmouth branch of the great western road. was FERNEBERGA in the Domesday Book and has a 12th century church.

inchampstead was FINCHAMSTEDE in the Berkshire folios of Domesday ook. It is also mentioned in the Anglo-Saxon Chronicle for 1098 and 1103 vhen "in the Summer a pool of blood welled up in Finchampstead out of soil". 'inchampstead was a bailiwick of Windsor Forest responsible for the red deer 'alks of Sandhurst, Bigshotte, Bearwood & Easthamptead. The main village as always been at Fair Green, some way from the church; a 3-day Whit fair vas granted in 1458 (Henry VI). The mound on which the church stands is kely to be an Iron-age fort which was used by the Romans.

Finchampstead, past present & future S Paulden Finchampstead Soc 1977 72pp

Finchampstead Church, St James, has Norman walls modernized with Tudo windows and pointed chancel arch. Features of interest: Norman or late Saxon font with a round stem of 1855; rare apsidal sanctuary; 1½ slit windows in the N wall of the nave; brick tower of 1720; brasses for Henry Hinde, Tudor Royal Purveyor, 1580 and Elizabeth Blighe d.1635; list of rectors from 1299. Samuel Marsh broke the quill in 1645 when obliged to sign the Solemn League and Covenant during the Civil War leaving the parish without a rector for 15 years.

Finchampstead Ridges were acquired by the National Trust in 1911 when John Walters III sold the Bearwood estate to aid the finances of the *The Times* The ridges are the edge of a gravel plateau (Terrace 8, Anglian) and the Blackwater Valley. The great size of the ancient river can be appreciated from here. Wellingtonia Avenue was planted around 1863 by John Walters II,

Firgrove Manor is Georgian and was built in 1736. Design and date suggest the architect was John James, who built Warbrook for himself in the village. The last Lords of the Manor lived here - the Copes who also owned Bramshill until they had to sell up in the 1930s. It is now flats.

Fleet was a 19th century new town that grew up on the almost uninhabited heath, common land of the tithing of Crookham in the Parish of Crondall. The first mention of the name is in the Crondall Customary of 1567, a *parcell of grounde now inclosed called Fleate Pond*. In the same document Widow Cawet had a croft near the pond, *Le Flete*. Fleet Pond Station interpolated in 1847 by the LSWR put the place on the map and the arrival of the army at Aldershot in 1855 provided jobs. Faster trains brought Fleet into the London commuter belt and the army spawned the Royal Aircraft Establishment - a major employer. All Saints Church was consecrated in 1862 and Fleet became a parish.

Fleet Pond is a nature reserve owned by the borough and maintained by the Fleet Pond Society to produce a diversity of habitats. Reed warblers, bitterns water rails and cormorants are regular visitors. The main feeder is the Gelvert Stream which drains the area around Cæsar's Camp. The pond was managed for fish stocks possibly from the Anglo Saxon era to the 19th century. In an indenture of 1505 the prior of St Swithun leased *La Flete* to William Gifford, Knight of Itchell for 23s 4d plus 100 fish per annum but retained the right to fish himself! The Latin text changed to English for the fish names : *pykes, tenches, perches, bremes* et *roches*. The railway split the pond. Fleet Pond Station was for London excursion trains - picnics in summer; skating in winter.

Frenchman's Oak, now propped up by scaffolding, is said to mark the limit to which paroled officers could walk on the London road from the great prisoner-of-war camp at Odiham during the Napoleonic Wars. The milestone next to it, 40 miles to London, was, presumably, the real mark.

Frimhurst was the home of the composer Dame Ethyl Smyth, 1858-1944, a Brahms pupil who is performed more in Germany than in Britain. Opposite it was Harmsworth's boat house 1901-38 for hiring rowing boats.

Frimley is not a Domesday Book village but the name gets its first airing in a charter of 933 as FREMELEY, suggesting derivation from Fremma's clearing. It was on the edge of Windsor Forest whose boundary was the Blackwater.

The **gas regulation station** steps down the pressure from the 44 bar of the national pipelines to 26, 7 and 2 bar for local distribution - analogous with an electricity transformer. The gas is filtered of dust and rust picked up in the pipes and heated to compensate for the cooling of decompression.

Gibraltar Barracks was founded in 1976 and replaced Southwood Barracks in Cove at a Royal Engineers Depot. The officers mess is Minley Manor.

artley Wintney is a large village whose charm lies in the jumble of styles and rge green with duck pond and cricket pitch - the Cricket Club dates from 770. It is not in the Domesday Book probably being then in the great Royal anor of Odiham. Its first mention is in a 13th century will bequeathing it to the istercian Priory. On dissolution the priory's estate went to Henry VIII's cellarer. was a coaching stop on the London to Exeter road with several inns and rriers. William Cobbett rode by in November 1821 and noted the planting of e oaks on the green. The old church, St Mary's, has a 19th century tower and ansepts appended to the 13th century nave and chancel. General "Hangman" awley and Field Marshall Viscount Alanbrooke are buried there. The new hurch, St John's, was built in 1870 when the village had moved down to the rnpike road. Before Camberley arose, the *White Lion* (now with Tea Rooms) as the first sign of habitation after Bagshot. General Walker had his Cavalier Q here in 1644 during the Civil War. The present building dates from about en. In 1776 it was the venue for the public meeting which first proposed the asingstoke Canal; as the eastern part would pass through heath, most of the terested landowners lived between Crookham and Basingstoke.

The Old Village of Hartley Wintney David Gorsky 5th ed 1995 HW Preserv Soc 73pp

awley was a hamlet and medieval tithing of Yateley. It had 16 dwellings in 567. The village was enclosed from the heath in 1817. Hawley Hill is the same lateau as Blackbushe. Hawley Woods and the heath extending to Fleet Pond ere part of Minley estate acquired by the War Department in 1936. They are sed by army for troop training, route marches, logistic support and attack. The ood and lake are used by film makers. The air strips are of unknown origin. hey are on the site of a balloon training station and may have been used for aining army spotter pilots. The author would welcome definite information.

awley Lake is used by the army for aquatic exercises. The Royal Engineers aining site is Hawley Hard. There are myths about the digging of the lake by WWI soldiers. The first OS 1" map, 1816, has a pond a furlong long in an area belled Peat Moor. The Yateley tithe map of 1846, has *Hawley Pond* without reeks, 560 yards long. The first OS 6" map, 1871, shows it at its present size nd shape. There was much landscaping in the late 1850s by Raikes Currie nd the dam may have been raised then.

lazeley Bottom is a hamlet of old cottages. It was originally home to the rtisans brought by Lord Zouche to construct the Bramshill house in 1605.

lazeley Heath is a private common on a ridge of plateau gravels (Terrace 6, nglian) between the farms of the Bramshill estate and those around it, on the ertiary Sands. Until 1850 there was a race course between Hazeley House nd Purdie's Farm, patronised by the many large houses nearby.

lazeley House is a late 18th century house, the family home for generations f the Singleton family from the time of George III until World War II (see the eltic cross in Mattingley churchyard). The garden is now a private arboretum.

ligh Curley is a promontory of the plateau (terrace 11, pre-Anglian) whose dge is Chobham Ridges on which runs the Maultway. The army tracks are ow used for training drivers on difficult terrain; until 2003 they were used for esting army vehicles. Maultway may derive from the Anglo-Saxon *molt*, sheep. armers on the more fertile soils of the North Downs may have sent flocks this ay for the summer to the great expanse of Surrey common land. Heatherside vas the name given to his house and 300 acres by the Swiss botanist Mongredien. He planted the Wellingtonias.

ock 15 of the Basingstoke Canal is the start of the Deepcut series of locks, 5-28, the main ascent, where the Basingstoke Canal climbs 29m/95 feet.

Long Valley has been a cavalry and tank training area. The test tracks are now used for cross country driver training and, by the Army Trials and Development Unit, for testing wheeled vehicles.

The Look Out is a recreational centre for Bracknell on Crown Estate land, managed as commercial forest.The area is a remnant of Windsor Forest which stretched north to the Thames, west to the Blackwater and south to the Downs

The **Martineau** Cottages were built by John Martineau 1834-1910 to improve the living conditions of farm workers. He was a household pupil of Charles Kingsley. Homilies are incised on the timbers. The houses are owned by a trust; there are several groups around Eversley and more in Suffolk.
John Martineau Pupil of Kingsley Violet Martineau 1922 Edward Arnold.

Mattingley is MATINGELEGE in the Domesday Book, a small manor with mill, in Holdshott Hundred. The church is a delightful timber frame building with oak pillars and herringbone brickwork - thought to be early Tudor but with aisles added and the roof cunningly extended in 1867. The bricks in the old part were made to fit the frame. It was a chapel of ease to Heckfield. The pope did not license it for burial of the dead until 1425. The Celtic cross in the churchyard marks the graves of the Singleton family of Hazeley House; nearby is a rare cob wall. *The History of a Hampshire Parish Heckfield & Mattingley* W J James 58pp

The **Military Museum** in Aldershot has an outdoor display of fighting vehicles and, inside, shows how the garrison developed - lots of uniforms. Museums of the Army Physical Training School and the Airborne Forces are nearby.

Mill Farm house was built in 1989 in 16th century style around the core of the old mill cottage. Its drive overlies the old Sandhurst road to the ford at the Tudor mill which stood until the 1880s. Yateley Mill is shown on John Norden's map of Windsor Forest of 1607. The road bridge was built in 1890.

Minley was the small Domesday Book manor of MINDESLEI in Holdshott Hundred held by Alfsi who was also lord of the manor of Mattingley. In the 18th century the estate belonged to the Tylneys, great Hampshire land-owners then to the Wyndhams. It was purchased by Raikes Currie, the banker, in the mid-1850s and it stayed in that family until the banking crisis of the 1920s. The War Department bought the estate as a training area in 1936.

Minley Manor - the house - was built 1858-60 on the site of an earlier house as a retirement home for Raikes Currie, the banker. The architect was Henry Clutton, author of *Domestic Architecture of France in the Middle Ages*, and the house is said to owe much to the Chateau de Blois. It was enlarged by Raikes' son and grandson. Mark Giraud, describes the house as "highly Victorian anarchy" in *Victorian Country Mansions*. When the War Department bought the estate, the house became part of the Staff College. When College extensions in Camberley were completed in the 1960s it was assigned to the Royal Engineers and is now the officers' mess. From time to time the gardens are open for public events. *The Manor of Minley* Brian A Myers 1984 38pp

Minley Warren was the home of Captain Blood ie the Jacobean fore-runner of the present house. Despite attempts on the Crown Jewels and the life of the Lord Lieutenant of Ireland, he was saved from execution and had his Irish lands restored to him by Charles II. Historians have hypothesized that while serving with the Roundheads he may have been aiding the king.

The **miniature railway** at Frimley Lodge Park started running in 1991. The 3000 feet of rails have three gauges 7¼", 5" & 3½". On 1st Sundays, March-November, the club is open to the public and train rides are given. 3rd Sundays are club members' running days. Wednesdays are maintenance days.

›ulsham Green, now a housing estate of Yateley, is mentioned as Mules
n, a boundary marker of Crondall in King Edgar's charter of 975.

›w Mill, hamlet and restaurant on the Blackwater are probably on the site of
e of the Domesday Book mills listed for Eversley. The mill building of 1577
s the wheel and grinding mechanism still in working order and it ground corn
til the beginning of the 20th century; it has also been a saw mill.

ne Mile Ride, now a tarmac road, was one of the paths cleared through
ndsor forest at the behest of George III; some say Queen Anne.

rth Camp was the part of the camp built north of the Basingstoke Canal
en the army came to Aldershot in 1855. The Iron Bridge over the canal
›laced an earlier pontoon bridge in 1870. Shops and banks sprang up on the
ge of the parish of Farnborough which also became known as North Camp
d was the main commercial area of Farnborough until the 1960s. The army
mp was originally tents and wooden huts but re-building in brick took place
the 1890s. Some of the brick buildings still stand but modern houses and
›cks have risen since the 1970s. North Camp Station is on the Reading to
ildford line which opened in 1849. It was only for army use until 1858.

liham has a delightful wide High Street with buildings of many periods all
ed in the book *Odiham High Street*. The settlement is very ancient. It was
›bably a Saxon royal hunting area and is first in the list in the Hampshire
ios of the Domesday Book - a great royal manor of 78½ hides. Conveniently
ed halfway between Winchester and Windsor or London, there are records
many visits by medieval kings. There seems to have been a palace before
d after King John's Castle was built. Parliament met in Odiham in 1303 and
zabeth I held Privy Council meetings here in 1569 and 1591.

liham Church, All Saints, is mainly of 13th century flint construction on the
e of the Saxon Domesday Book church but much restored. Points of interest:
piscina which may be Saxon; the 14th century pillars of the 3-arched north
le contrasting with 15th century pillars in the 4-arched south aisle; several
asses now on the walls, one above the lectern of 1498 for William Goode,
est; the heavily carved Jacobean pulpit; the RAF window in the tower arch.
o French gravestones outside the south wall date from the Napoleonic
ars. Outside the gate are the stocks. The pest house, at the SW corner of
graveyard, built under a bequest of 1625 was an isolation hospital
rticularly associated with plague. It was used as an almshouse, 1780-1978.

liham Wharf opened in 1793 and grew to 3 acres with warehouses, offices
d workshops near the car park. Land owners met at *The George* in Odiham
finalise the sale of land for the canal in 1788. The sons of John Pinkerton,
canal's engineer, lived in Odiham to supervise the building.

e **oil pipelines**, indicated by wayside marks, are owned by ESSO and were
ilt in the 1960s. They run from the refinery at Fawley and branch near Alton
Heathrow and Gatwick. The 10" pipe carries only aviation fuel. The 12" pipe
rries different products at different times for distribution in the London area.

›ark pale noted on a map may be visible on the ground as a mound which
arked the boundary of the emparked area and originally had high wooden
lings. Parks were private enclosures for deer keeping licensed by the crown,
›stly medieval in origin. The deer were captured by them driving against the
ice (reserves for pursuit hunting were chases). Many were disparked several
nturies ago but the name lingered. Houses with *Park* in the name hark back
emparkment real or imaginary. The real ones were often manor houses.
The Bishop of Winchester's Deer Parks 1200-1400 Proc Hants Arch Soc Vol 43 1988

Pirbright is not a Domesday Book village but was probably cut from Woking Manor by Henry I for his son Robert, Duke of Gloucester. The marriage portion of Katherine of Aragon included Pirbright. The Manor House dates from the 16th century but there are records of a house in 1302; part of its moat is still visible. The mill, next-door, ground corn until the 1930s. The church, St Michael and All Angels, is Georgian but there was a church as early as 1200, deduced from a charter signed as witness by Jordan, parson of Pirefricth (facsimile in church). The grave of the explorer Sir Henry Morton Stanley, 1841-1904, is in the churchyard. *The Day before Yesterday - the Story of Pirbright* Helen Yool

Pirbright Lodge was the home of Admiral John Byron, 1723-86, who explored the Pacific rather badly, fought a French fleet rather easily and became a grandfather poetically. As midshipman he was shipwrecked in Patagonia for six years; story has it that he set off to retire there but, coming to Pirbright, found it wild enough and stayed. The lane was the Chertsey-Farnham coach road.

The **pillbox**es were part of the GHQ line between the Thames and Severn estuaries to protect London and the Midlands in the Second World War. The line linked geographical barriers such as the North Downs, River Wey and Basingstoke Canal. Pillboxes and tank traps were at weak points .
Pillboxes - a study of UK defences 1940 H Wills Secker & Warburg 1985 98pp

Plateaus - Ice Age terraces of the Blackwater: see box on p 63.

Pyestock research station was the National Gas Turbine Establishment 1946-91, now part of the Farnborough aviation complex. It tests engines for aircraft and ships and was central to the early development of jet engines. The engine was first proposed at Farnborough in 1926. Frank Whittle, an RAF officer, started his designs in 1927 and patented them in 1930. Power Jet Ltd was formed in Lutterworth to develop Whittle's engines and the prototype flew in 1941. Farnborough designed an engine in 1939 which flew in 1942. The site was founded in 1941 to bring together the Farnborough and Power Jet teams.

Queen's Parade, now used for sport, is was where Queen Victoria reviewed the troops. There was a race course around it in the 1870's before Tweseldown was laid out. It was used for trials of early observation balloons for the army.

Railways of the area: see the box on page 29

The **redoubts**, humps on the heath, were defences for guns at the great army training exercises of 1792. About 7000 soldiers participated, infantry, cavalry and artillery. George III inspected and the Reading Mercury reported 200 000 spectators were present at the arrival of the regiments. The camp was lampooned in the London theatres. *Bastions of Berkshire Berks CC 12pp*

Riseley Mill is the lowest of eight mills on the Whitewater River - late 18th century in origin. It ceased to operate when the mechanism failed in 1910.
Journey down the Whitewater Anne Pitcher 1982 Whitewater Valley Preserv. Soc 63pp

Rivers: see box on page 3: Loddon, Blackwater, Whitewater, Hart

Rotherwick was part of the large, royal Saxon manor of Odiham. The name most likely derives from the Saxon *hrither*, cattle, so this may have been the dairy farm for the Royal estate. It became part of Greywell Manor when that was detached from Odiham around 1240 and a manor in its own right in the 16th century which was bought by Richard Tylney in 1629. The village hall, despite its antiquated timber-framed form, was built in 1932 as a memorial for the son of Henry de Forrest, an American, who had leased Tylney Hall for shooting visits. The church was a chapel of rest to Heckfield parish church. The late 13th century chancel is the oldest part. The 15th century nave had timber frame walls (like Mattingley) which can be seen in the gables internally.

rsens - see box on page 55.

r Henry Morton **Stanley**, 1841-1904, of "Dr Livingstone, I presume" fame tired to Furze Hill in Pirbright Parish, hence the African names on OS maps. ought up in a Welsh workhouse he fought in the American civil war and came a *New York Herald* journalist. His great *coup* was the expedition to ntral Africa to find Livingstone who had been "lost" trying to establish that ke Tanganyika was the source of the Nile; they met at Ujiji, November 1871. e continued Livingstone's work in a second expedition, following the Lualaba ver down to the Atlantic to find it was the Congo, not the Nile. Employed by e Belgian king to set up a chain of trading stations Stanley became the eator of the Congo (now Zaire) and a catalyst for the carve up of Africa by e European powers. His last expedition saved Emin Pasha from the Mahdi.

Stanley (Vol 1) *Making of an African Explorer* Frank McLynn 1989 Constable 411pp
Stanley (Vol 2) *Sorcerer's Apprentice* Frank McLynn 1991 Constable 499pp

rrey Hill has a flat top (Terrace 11, pre-Anglian) traversed by the county undary. The reservoir holds 42 000m3/900 000 gallons and serves Yateley, andhurst & Crowthorne and parts of Camberley & Fleet.

vallowfield Church, All Saints, was re-built in 1256 by the Lord of the Manor, r John le Despenser, replacing an earlier one which was a chapel-of-ease to infield. Points of interest: Backhouse family pew of 1690, the 14th century issor bracing of the bell turret, a disused Norman doorway of around 1120; asses of 1442 and 1554; the grave (near the kissing gate)of Mary Mitford, '87-1855, author of *Our Village*, who lived in the parish.

vallowfield is SWALFELLE in the Domesday Book. The first record of a park as in 1316 when it seems to have been used as a stud farm. The Park was me to many noble families in Norman times and subsequently. The present use was built by Talman around 1670 for the 2nd Earl of Clarendon. Thomas tt, grandfather of the prime minister, Pitt the Elder, bought the estate in 1719 it of the £125,000 he received for the sale of a diamond acquired when he as Governor of Madras (inspiring Wilkie Collins' *Moonstone*). Sir Henry issell bought the estate in 1820 and it remained in that family until 1965. The rdens are open on certain week days during the summer months.

Swallowfield and its owners Lady Russell Longmans 1901 362pp

ie **trig point** near the Look Out, designated Pudding Hill, was built in 1950 at cost of £15-14s. It was a second order survey point in the third triangulation Britain, initiated in 1936. Tree cover must have been absent at the time.

ie **telecommunications** tower belongs to BT and is 100m tall. It was built out 1965 for colour television distribution to transmitters when copper cable is unable to handle frequencies up to 11 gigaHertz. Many of the antennae on e lattice-work belong to site sharers who are able to rent space on the tower.

ndry Pond is a quiet stretch of water with kingfishers, sandpipers and rons. The causeway bridge was built for the carriages of Sir Henry Paulet St hn when the canal cut his normal route from Dogmersfield Park. The pond is enlarged as during the landscaping of the park.

veseldown Racecourse was the army racecourse laid out soon after the my settled in Aldershot in 1855. It is now leased to a private company and is ed for point-to-point racing and other equestrian events.

arbrook is currently an IBM training centre. The house and garden were laid t for himself in 1724 by John James, a pupil of Christopher Wren.

elsh Drive is an ancient drove road, the route by which drovers from Wales ought meat on the hoof to medieval markets at Blackwater and London.

The **Wellington Statue** arrived in this position in 1885 - 40 tons of bronze from guns captured at Waterloo. It was always controversial. There were objections to commemorating Wellington when it was erected in 1846 and when it was removed from Hyde Park corner for road widening in 1882. Currently objectors believe such a splendid statue should stand in a more public place.

The Wellington Military Memorial 1885-1985 Tim Childerhouse Southern Books 198

Wharfenden Lake is the site of the Lakeside Country Club and was the HQ of ENSA during World War II. "Every night something awful" said the soldiers.

Wildmoor Heath is greatly valued in Berkshire as one of its few heaths. It is an assemblage of various bits of land mainly heath and bog put together as a reserve managed by Berkshire, Buckinghamshire & Oxfordshire Wildlife Trust.

Winchfield Church, St Mary's, is Norman. The chancel arch and south door c about 1150 are elaborately decorated and well-preserved. The nave was Gothicized with larger pointed windows in Victorian times but the chancel retains its Norman form with narrow windows (some restored) and thick walls. Winchfield was gifted to Chertsey Abbey in a charter of 675 but the Domesday Book contradicts this. The modern village is far away near the railway station.

The **Windle** Brook issues from Rapley Lake and drains the eastern heights of Bagshot Heath. After Windlesham it becomes the Mill Bourne in Chobham.

Windlesham became a village only in the 19th century. Before that, perhaps reflecting its forest origin, it was scattered hamlets, one of which was Bagshot The Great Western Road (now the A30) formed the northern boundary of the parish. Windlesham is not in the Domesday Book. There were several early land holdings. One formed part of Edward the Confessor's endowment of Westminster Abbey. One was given to Broomhill Convent early in the Middle Ages. South of the village was W Froman & Sons' nursery supplying trees and shrubs to the London area. This began with 15 acres in 1894 but was 250 acres by 1911 and employed 60 men in the 1930s. When the owner retired in 1981 it was sold in lots some of which became the arboretum. The church, St John, the Baptist, was rebuilt in 1874 but has the medieval nave as the south aisle and the tower of 1838. Church documents date back to 1189.

The **Wishmoor Stone**, a sarsen, was *Wysshemorestone* in the perambulation of Godley Hundred of 1446. It appears to mark where the county boundary takes off from the Wish Stream over Surrey Hill. Five civil parishes meet there Winkfield, Easthampstead, Crowthorne, Frimley & Camberley and Windlesham

The **Wish** Stream drains part of Bagshot Common. It joins the Blackwater nea the Meadows roundabout and is the county boundary throughout its length.

Yateley was probably part of Domesday Book Cove which found itself in the medieval parish of Yateley. From the 10th century it was Winchester church property so many old records survive. The houses of the medieval village - seven in a rental of 1287 - probably lay on the old Reading road opposite the green and the "big house" was probably on the site of the present Yateley Manor School near the church. The parish had a scattering of hamlets and houses and 20th century village resulted from filling the gaps. The population is estimated to have been about 300 in 1287, was 470 in 1801 and is almost 21,000 in 2005. The church, St Peters, was badly burnt (arson) in 1979 when the Norman arches collapsed. The timber tower of about 1450 survived. The damage enabled archæologists to investigate the north wall which was found to have a blocked Anglo-Saxon window (now restored). The sarsen L of the porch at the NW corner of the A-S church may indicate a pre-Christian religious site. *Yateley, a mediæval village* Derek Doherty Yateley Society 1982 21pp